A

ENGLISH AS A SECOND LANGUAGE

IN ENGLISH

Bruno Gattuso
Benoit Jaret
Maria Lee-Arpino
Isabelle Sauvé

Geneviève Roussin

Project Direction:
Virginie Krysztofiak
Paul Ste-Marie

Éditions Grand Duc ▪ HRW
Groupe Éducalivres inc.
955, rue Bergar, Laval (Québec) H7L 4Z6
Téléphone : (514) 334-8466 ▪ Télécopie : (514) 334-8387
InfoService : 1 800 567-3671

Depuis le 1er avril 2004, les Éditions HRW affichent
une nouvelle raison sociale, soit Éditions Grand Duc ▪ HRW.

Acknowledgements

The publisher wishes to thank the following people for their comments and suggestions during the development of this project:

Mr. Alain Audet, teacher, École secondaire Mgr A.-M. Parent, C. S. Marie-Victorin
Mrs. Julie Bourdages, teacher, Collège Notre-Dame-de-Lourdes
Mrs. Marjorie Carrière, teacher, École le Sommet, C. S. des Premières-Seigneuries
Mrs. Julie Charland, teacher, Les Ateliers de langues du Collège Saint-Charles-Garnier
Mrs. Suzan Faucher, teacher, École du Triolet, C. S. de la Région-de-Sherbrooke
Mrs. Laurie Fréchette, teacher, École Jacques-Rousseau, C. S. Marie-Victorin
Mr. Brian Gibson, teacher, École Massey-Vanier, C. S. du Val-des-Cerfs
Ms. Manon Jarvis, teacher, École secondaire de la Montée–Pavillon Saint-François, C. S. de la Région-de-Sherbrooke
Mr. Marc Laflamme, teacher, École secondaire de Rochebelle–Pavillon Gilles-Vigneault, C. S. des Découvreurs
Mrs. Johanne Lemire, teacher, École du Triolet, C. S. de la Région-de-Sherbrooke
Mrs. Denise Mc Grath, teacher, École secondaire de Rochebelle–Pavillon Gilles-Vigneault, C. S. des Découvreurs
Mrs. Geneviève Roussin, teacher, Séminaire de Sherbrooke

We acknowledge the financial support of the Government of Canada through the Book Publishing Industry Development Program (BPIDP) for our publishing activities.

ILLUSTRATIONS: Claude Bordeleau, Yves Boudreau, Jérôme Mercier.

PRODUCT CODE 3391
ISBN 0-03-928767-X

Legal Deposit – 1st Quarter, 2005
Bibliothèque nationale du Québec, 2005
National Library of Canada, 2005

Printed in Canada

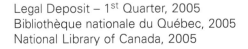
1 2 3 4 5 6 7 8 9 0 II 4 3 2 1 0 9 8 7 6 5

Table of Contents

Introduction

Learning and Evaluation Situations

Reference Toolkit

Letter To Students

Learning English as a second language helps you communicate with people who speak English in Quebec, across Canada and around the world.

It makes it possible for you to understand and share lots of information and enjoy entertainment in the English language. Just think about all the media resources (television, music, radio, books and magazines, as well as the Internet) you will be able to look at, listen to or read.

With the help of *Kick-off in English,* your teacher and your classmates will assist you to develop your English competencies. But you will have to interact, participate actively and be involved in the learning process every step of the way. For a good "kick-off," you need to:

- Take some risks when you interact;
  Don't be afraid to make mistakes when you speak.

- Ask for help when you don't understand something;
  Be responsible for your learning in the classroom.

- Encourage your classmates and act cooperatively;
  Good teamwork and encouragement is always A+.

Also, to use this textbook effectively, you need to know how it works. Read the following pages, *Kick-off*–An Overview, to learn more.

Have a great year in English!

The Authors

Kick-off – An Overview

This Student Book is organized to help you learn English and make you feel competent when you carry out different activities. It proposes nine separate units (learning and evaluation situations), each based on a special theme. Content is presented in such a way as to help you develop your competencies.

UNIT STRUCTURE

Unit Opener

At the beginning of each unit, you will find two pages that introduce the unit's theme and provide an outline of what you will learn in that unit. You will begin each unit with a simple, enjoyable activity designed to activate your prior knowledge and vocabulary on the theme.

■ PREPARATION

Activities

The next pages of each unit present two or three activities that will help you prepare to learn new material. These pages are always structured in the same way:

Instructions and questions explaining the activity are always written on the sides of the pages in a *notebook* box.

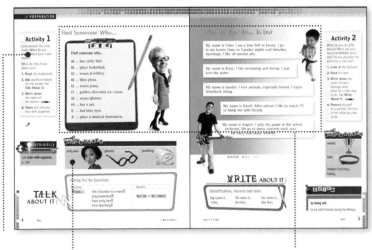

Vocabulary box.

The remainder of the pages are filled with texts and pictures. Any words or expressions printed in blue are defined in the Vocabulary and the Idiom boxes.

Steps

In this part of each unit, you will expand and practice new language related to the theme by means of reading and listening activities. You will explore different text types and strategies and interact orally with your classmates and teacher. Each step is designed to help you reinvest your understanding of texts.

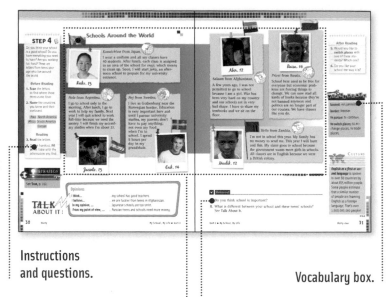

Instructions and questions.

Texts and pictures.

Vocabulary box.

Reinvest instructions and questions.

Projects, Getting Started

This last part of the unit presents activities especially designed to prepare and carry out different projects. The Reinvest box outlines important content you will need to reinvest in your project by writing or producing texts. All the *Extra Carrying out* steps can also be treated as enrichment activities.

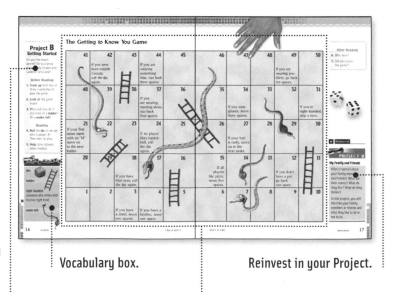

Vocabulary box.

Reinvest in your Project.

Instructions and questions.

Texts and pictures.

VI

Wrap-up page

Your Project Presentation outlines the last details you should think about so as to be ready to show your project.

Your Portfolio reminds you to update your portfolio with all the significant work and handouts you completed during the unit.

You will also find special features in each unit.

Models and tips on how to structure your oral interactions.

Writing tips to help you structure short writing tasks.

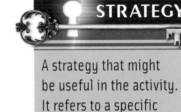

A strategy that might be useful in the activity. It refers to a specific page of the *Strategies* section at the end of the textbook.

CULTURE

Definitions of expressions that might be difficult to understand at first.

Extra information on a topic related to a text, the theme of the unit, or English culture around the world.

Riddles, jokes and funny cartoons related to the theme of the unit.

Explanations of Icons

This icon indicates a listening activity.

This icon indicates that you need a handout to complete the activity.

This icon indicates that you have to use a notebook to write words, sentences or paragraphs.

THE REFERENCE TOOLKIT

The end of your Student Book contains a Reference Toolkit that is useful in many ways. It has three different sections.

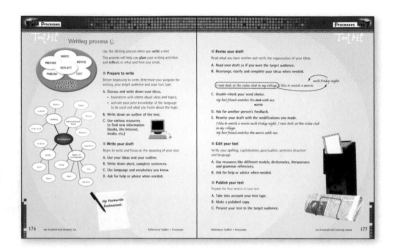

Processes

These pages explain how to use the different phases of the response, writing and production processes. You will especially explore the *response process* in the Carrying Out activities of the units. You will experience the *writing process* and the *production process* in your projects.

Strategies

This section gives you models of how to use different communication and learning strategies. As you progress through the units, the *Strategy* box (see previous page) will refer you to specific strategies you will find helpful in the activities.

Vocabulary

This section includes a short dictionary of all the words and expressions explained in the *Vocabulary* and *Idiom* boxes.

Steve

Brian

Karyn

IN THIS UNIT

You Will...

- get to know your classmates and discover what they like;

- read and listen to teens describing what they like and their favourite leisure activity;

- complete some amusing personality tests;

- describe yourself, your family and friends.

Text Types

Look at, read and/or listen to...

e-mail, a teen magazine and a magazine article, a timeline, questionnaires, a radio show, a board game, maps and surveys.

Strategies

- infer with visual clues and cognates;

- pay selective attention.

Projects

Write or produce one of the following projects:

- *Home Sweet Home;*

- *My Family and Friends;*

- *The Time Capsule.*

1. **Look** at the picture.

2. **Answer** the questions.

   A) Who is listening to music?

   B) Who is not having fun?

   C) Who is sitting down?

   D) Who is playing ball?

   E) Who has long hair?

   F) Who is not wearing a jacket?

   G) Who is smiling?

   H) Who looks cool?

Find Someone Who...

Activity 1

Look around the classroom. What do you know about your classmates?

What do they know about you?

1. **Read** the statements.

2. **Ask** questions based on the survey. See **Talk About It.**

3. **Write down** the name of the person. ◄▒▒▒►

4. **Share** the information with a partner.

Find someone who...

A) ... has curly hair.

B) ... plays basketball.

C) ... wears jewellery.

D) ... likes pizza.

E) ... wears jeans.

F) ... prefers chocolate ice cream.

G) ... wears glasses.

H) ... has a pet.

I) ... has blue eyes.

J) ... plays a musical instrument.

STRATEGY

See **Infer with cognates,** p. 190.

Vocabulary

curly hair: glasses: jewellery:

TALK ABOUT IT!

Asking Yes/No Questions

QUESTIONS		ANSWERS
Do you...	like chocolate ice cream?	
	play basketball?	Yes I do. or No. I don't.
	have curly hair?	
	wear jewellery?	

What Do You Like... To Do?

My name is Chen. I am a blue belt in karate. I go to my karate class on Tuesday nights and Saturday mornings. I like all martial arts.

My name is Rosie. I like swimming and diving. I just love the water.

My name is Sandra. I love animals, especially horses. I enjoy horseback riding.

My name is David. After school, I like to watch TV or hang out with friends.

My name is Angelo. I play the guitar in the school orchestra. We go to many concerts each year. We have won many awards.

Activity 2

What do you do after school? What are your favourite **leisure** activities? Do you practice the activities in the text?

1. **Look at** the pictures.

2. **Read** the text.

3. **Write down** the name of each teenager and what he or she likes to do. See **Write About It.**

4. **Present** yourself to a partner. Tell him or her what you like to do.

VOCABULARY

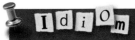

award:

belt:

leisure: free time, hobby.

WRITE ABOUT IT!

Identification, interest and taste

My name is ...	His name is...	Her name is...
I like...	He likes...	She likes...

Idiom

to hang out.

to be with friends doing fun things.

STEP 1

Do you have a penpal or an epal? Would you like to have one?

Before reading

1. What kind of text is it?
   • a Web page?
   • a letter?
   • an email?

2. Who sent this text?

3. Who received this text?

Reading

4. **Read** the text.

5. **Find** out what Franco likes and dislikes.

After reading

6. Do you have the same preferences as Franco?

Tell Me What You Like

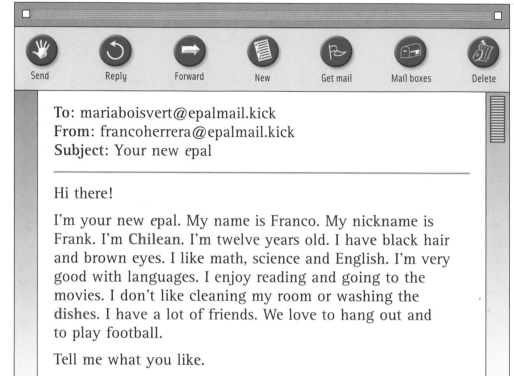

To: mariaboisvert@epalmail.kick
From: francoherrera@epalmail.kick
Subject: Your new epal

Hi there!

I'm your new epal. My name is Franco. My nickname is Frank. I'm **Chilean**. I'm twelve years old. I have black hair and brown eyes. I like math, science and English. I'm very good with languages. I enjoy reading and going to the movies. I don't like cleaning my room or washing the **dishes**. I have a lot of friends. We love to hang out and to play football.

Tell me what you like.

Write to me soon ☺.
Hasta la vista,

Frank

vocabulary

Chilean: from the country of Chile.

dishes:

In Canada and the United States, *football* is usually called *soccer*.

CULTURE

▼ Reinvest

7. Ask a partner if he or she has the same preferences as you.

   See **Talk About It** on next page.

Answering Yes/No Questions

QUESTIONS

ANSWERS

Do you like...?
Do you have...?

Yes, I do.

Yes, very much.

Yes, a lot.

Yes, sometimes.

No, I don't.

No, not much.

No, not really.

No, not at all.

Interest and tastes

I | love / am fond of / like | ... my pet animal.

I | enjoy / appreciate | ... math and languages.

I | love / like | ... to read and to play football.

I | don't like / dislike / hate | ... to wash the dishes.

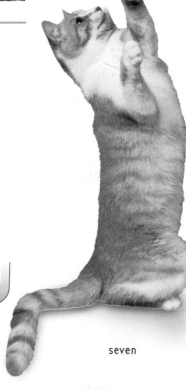

STEP 2 📝

Do you worry about your accent in English? Did you notice that many people speak English with an accent? Can you understand them?

Before listening

1. **Look at** the pictures.

2. How do you think these teens spend their time?

3. Are their leisure activities different from yours?

Listening

4. **Listen to** The Phone-in Show.

5. **Find** out who is speaking on the phone.

6. Can you hear the different accents?

7. Can you understand the teenagers on the phone?

Sandra, from Ottawa, Canada.

Mark, from Brisbane, Australia.

Shamini, from New Delhi, India

STRATEGY

See **Pay selective attention,** p. 184.

CULTURE

A **sari** is the traditional clothing of Hindu women. It's usually made of cotton or silk.

Bollywood movies are romantic movies filmed in India. They are extravagant and usually contain songs and dances.

Billy Joe, from Dallas, Texas (USA).

Yoko, from Osaka, Japan.

Philip, from London, England.

After Listening

8. Which of these activities do you like best?

9. Which of these teens would make a good penpal or epal?

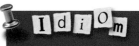

to move on.

to do something else.

that sounds great!

it's wonderful!

CULTURE

Rugby is originally a British ball game. It resembles American football, but it is physically much rougher. The first recorded rugby game was played in London, in 1175.

▼ **Reinvest**

10. On your handout, **write down** what you like and what you don't like about these teens' activities.

The Colour of Your Personality

STEP 3

Look around you! There are colours everywhere. People **believe** that colours express our personality and our feelings. Colours also have different meanings in different cultures.

Before Reading

1. **Look** at the colours on pages 10 and 11.

2. What is your favourite colour?

Reading

3. **Read** the text about your favourite colour.

Red

People who like red are passionate and loving. They are emotional and demonstrative. They are very exciting friends. They like to have fun. They dislike being contradicted because it makes them **angry** very quickly. Red is the colour of power and of love. In China, it is the colour of good luck. In South Africa, red is the colour for funerals.

Yellow

People who like yellow are happy and **cheerful**. They are **hopeful** and optimistic. They always look at the good side of things. They like to have a good time with friends. They dislike **fights** and **quarrels**. Yellow is the colour of peace and hope. In India, people wear yellow to celebrate the festival of spring.

Blue

People who like blue are cool, calm and relaxed. They are confident, intelligent and strong. They are loyal and **faithful** friends. They like stability. They dislike change and last-minute things. In ancient Rome, public servants wore blue. In China, blue is the colour for little girls.

STRATEGY

See **Infer with cognates**, p. 190.

Green People who like green are youthful and lively. They like sports and the outdoors. Like "blue people", they can also be cool and calm. They are very adaptable people. They like harmony and stability. They also prefer order. They don't like to lose. Green is the national colour of Ireland.

Purple, Violet People who like purple are very spiritual people. They may also believe in the supernatural. They are very brave. They are independent and original. They have a lot of imagination and love to create. They dislike big crowds. Purple was the favourite colour of the Egyptian queen, Cleopatra.

Black People who like black are very mysterious. They are sophisticated and elegant. They love to travel and discover things. They are good at puzzles and riddles. They dislike noise. They don't like to communicate their feelings. In China, black is the colour for little boys.

▼ Reinvest

7. Team up with classmates who chose your colour.

8. Describe your team to the other students. See Talk About It.

> We are the colour team.
>
> It means that we are adjectives. We like ....
> We dislike ....

TALK ABOUT IT!

After reading

4. Does the text about your favourite colour reflect your personality?

   Write down the characteristics that represent you.

5. **Find** other classmates who chose the same colour as you.

6. Do you believe that certain personality traits can be represented by colours?

VOCABULARY

angry:

to believe: to think something is true or real.

cheerful: happy.

crowd: a large group of people.

faithful: loyal, true.

fight: battle, conflict.

hopeful: optimistic.

quarrel: dispute.

youthful: young, fresh.

How do we learn things?
What is your style
of learning?

Before Reading

1. **Pay attention** to
the **icons** and
the subtitles.

2. What types of intelli-
gence do you think
you use?

3. **Fill in** the questions
in your handout.

Reading

4. **Read** the paragraph
that matches your
answers on the
handout.

After reading

5. Does the paragraph
describe your style
of learning well?

6. Do you have more
than one style
of learning?

What's Your Intelligence Type?

According to theorist Howard Gardner, there is no single intelligence type. In order to explain how we learn, he defines different types of intelligence.

Spatial Intelligence

Spatial intelligence is about using pictures, maps and directions. We use spatial intelligence when we do puzzles, when we build things, when we find our way using a map or when we are in a new place. For example: photographers, architects and painters all use spatial intelligence.

Musical Intelligence

Musical intelligence is about using musical ability. We use musical intelligence when we remember songs, when we sing and when we play musical instruments or appreciate or criticize music. For example: musicians, singers, dancers and music lovers all use musical intelligence.

STRATEGY

See **Pay selective attention**, p. 184.

Why is the math book sad?

Because it has so many problems.

Linguistic Intelligence

Linguistic intelligence is about using language. We use linguistic intelligence when we read, when we write, when we tell stories and jokes and whenever we try to convince people about something. For example: writers, teachers, politicians and lawyers all use linguistic intelligence.

Logical/ Mathematic Intelligence

Logical/mathematical intelligence is about reasoning. We use logical/mathematical intelligence when we work with formulas and numbers, when we solve problems and when we play games like chess. For example: scientists, engineers and inventors all use logical/mathematical intelligence.

Interpersonal Intelligence

Interpersonal intelligence is about relationships. We use interpersonal intelligence when we do teamwork and cooperative work and when we try to understand the opinions and needs of other people. For example: teachers, psychologists, team leaders and social workers all use interpersonal intelligence.

Kinesthetic Intelligence

Kinesthetic intelligence is about movement. We use kinesthetic intelligence when we do sports, when we dance and when we use body language. For example: athletes, dancers, actors and carpenters all use kinesthetic intelligence.

▼ ▐ Reinvest

7. Write down a short description of your style of learning. See Write About it. ✏️➡️

WRITE ABOUT IT!

I use intelligence type when I ....

Project A
Getting Started

Where do you live? Is everything in your house always in its **proper** place? Is your room as clean as your parents would like?

Before Reading

1. **Look at** the picture.

2. Is everything in the **proper** place?

Reading

3. **Name** the different rooms in the house.

4. **Read** the **Word Bank.**

5. **Name** as many of the **appliances**, pieces of furniture and other objects you can see in the picture.

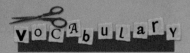

appliance: any machine used to do a particular job in and around the house.

misplaced: in the wrong place.

proper: correct.

The object(s) is/are in the room.

Example: The toaster is in the living room.

TALK ABOUT IT!

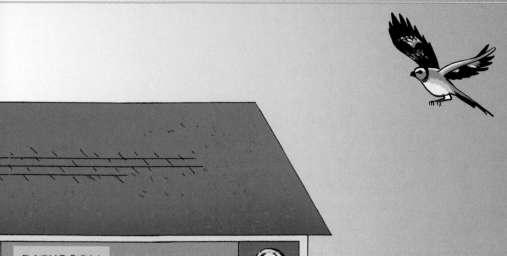

After reading

6. Find the misplaced objects in the house.

7. Tell a classmate in which rooms the **misplaced** objects are. See **Talk About It.**

word bank

dishwasher

toaster

cat

dishes

tiger

lamp

toothbrush

shower

sofa

birdcage

coffee machine

television

CD

BATHROOM

LIVING ROOM

HALLWAY

▼ **Reinvest**

Home Sweet Home   **PROJECT A**

What is special about your home? Which is your favourite room? What is your life at home like? Do you have a pet?

In this project, you will describe your home, any special objects found in your home and all the people and pets living with you.

The Getting to Know You Game

Project B
Getting Started

Do you like board games? Do you know how to play Snakes and Ladders? Let's play!

Before Reading

1. **Team up** with two or three classmates to play the game.

2. **Look at** the game board.

3. **What will you do** if you land on a **ladder**? On a **snake tail**?

Reading

4. **Roll** the **die** to decide who is player #1. Then start to play.

5. **Help** other players when needed.

vocabulary

die:

ladder:

right-handed: someone who writes with his/her right hand.

snake tail:

41	42 If you were born outside Canada, roll the die again.	43	44 If you are wearing something blue, run back three spaces.	45
40	39	38	37 If you are wearing running shoes, run back four spaces.	36
21 If your first name starts with an "M" move on to the next ladder.	22	23	24 If no player likes basketball, roll the die again.	25
20	19	18	17	16
1	2	3 If you have blue eyes, roll the die again.	4	5
		If you have a sister, move two spaces.	If you have a brother, move one space.	

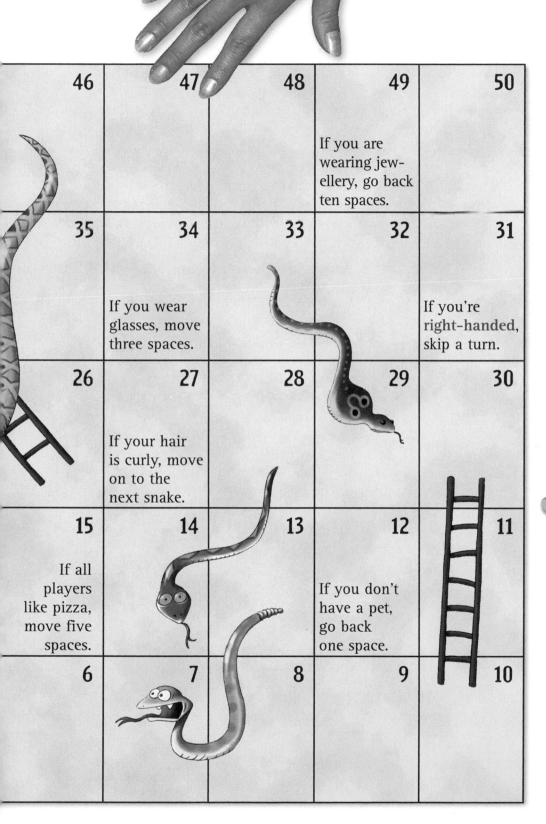

46	47	48	49 If you are wearing jew-ellery, go back ten spaces.	50
35	34 If you wear glasses, move three spaces.	33	32	31 If you're right-handed, skip a turn.
26	27 If your hair is curly, move on to the next snake.	28	29	30
15 If all players like pizza, move five spaces.	14	13	12 If you don't have a pet, go back one space.	11
6	7	8	9	10

After Reading

6. Who won?

7. Did you enjoy the game?

▼ Reinvest

PROJECT B

My Family and Friends

What is special about your family members and friends? What are their names? What do they like? What do they dislike?

In this project, you will describe your family members or friends and what they like to do or not to do.

Time Warp

Project C
Getting Started

Do you know what your parents or grandparents liked when they were teenagers? Do you know what happened then?

Before Reading

1. **Look at** the pictures.

2. **Can you recognize** some of them?

Reading

3. **Read** the text.

4. **Match** each picture to the appropriate decade.

5. **Compare** your answers to those of a classmate.

After reading

6. **Which decade do** you know best?

THE 60s — This is the decade of the Woodstock Rock Festival and "peace and love." People protest against the war in Vietnam. Musicians like *The Beatles, The Rolling Stones* and *The Doors* are very popular. Man walks on the Moon for the first time.

The 70s — The blockbuster *Star Wars* comes out in 1977. The *Bee Gees* and disco music are extremely popular. Men grow long hair and moustaches. People protest against nuclear bombs and the Cold War between the USA and the USSR. John Lennon writes the song *Give Peace a Chance*.

The 80s — Punk and New Wave music is very popular. The first audio CD arrives in music stores. TV channels show music videos. *Gremlins* and *Teenage Mutant Ninja Turtles* are Top-10 movies.

The 90s — Between 1989 and 1991, most Eastern European countries and Russia turn away from Communism. Video consoles and computer games are becoming more and more popular. People browse the Internet and chat online. The TV show *The Simpsons* comes out in the early 90s.

▼ Reinvest

A Time Capsule

PROJECT C

What is representative of you and your life today? What if you put something special in a box that says something about who you are? What if someone should find your box in 2100?

In this project, you will team up, find and describe objects that are representative of you and what you like.

Your Project Presentation

- Did you work individually or in teams?
- Was each task you had to do clear?
- How much time did you spend on your project?
- Do you need more practice to prepare for your presentation?
- Do you think the audience will appreciate your project?
- What do you think will captivate them?
- Did you ask for advice from other students or your teacher in order to finish your project?

It's time to present your project.

Take risks and speak clearly to keep your classmates' and teacher's attention.

Your Portfolio

In this unit, you experienced a lot of different activities related to you, your personality, your classmates and other teens your age. You learned to use some new words and expressions; you learned to use new strategies when reading and listening to texts.

Be sure to put the following items in your portfolio:

- The *In this Unit* handout, to self-evaluate your learning in relation to oral interactions, texts and strategies.
- All the notes and short texts you wrote in the Reinvest section at the end of some of the activities.
- The *Vocabulary* and *Language* handouts that you completed.
- The *Evaluation* handouts you completed.
- Any texts, documents, pictures or handouts you used during your project.

1. Read these clues.

A) The room in which you eat.

B) The place where you put your coat and books.

C) The place where you can run.

D) You can find them in the library.

E) You use it to be in the right class at the right time.

F) A world map is essential to this class.

G) The class in which you are now.

H) Many students take it to come to school.

I) You keep your pens and pencils in it.

J) The place illustrated in the picture.

IN THIS UNIT

You Will...

- solve a make-believe treasure hunt at school;

- discuss your preferences about your old school and your new school;

- reflect on school rules, schedules and extra-curricular activities;

- read and listen to teens describing what they like and dislike about school.

Text Types

Look at, read and/or listen to...

schedules, teen magazine articles, maps, instructions, comic strips, an advertising booklet, letters and e-mails.

Strategies

- skim;

- infer with visual clues;

- scan;

- compare.

Projects

Write or produce one of the following projects:

- *The School Quiz;*

- *My Dream Schedule;*

- *A Secondary Cycle One Survival Guide.*

2. Find the answers in the Word Bank.

word bank				
school bus	geography	hallway	pencil case	books
cafeteria	locker	gymnasium	schedule	English

Raiders of the Lost Book

Activity 1

Are you a good detective? Try to find out where the lost book is.

1. **Look at** the school map.

2. **Answer** the questions in the school map with the **Word Bank.**

3. **Read** the fewest **hints** possible to find out where the lost book is.

4. Where is the missing book?

Hint #1
The lost book is far away from the locker room.

Hint #2
The English classroom will bring you closer.

Hint #3
You will smell food when you are close.

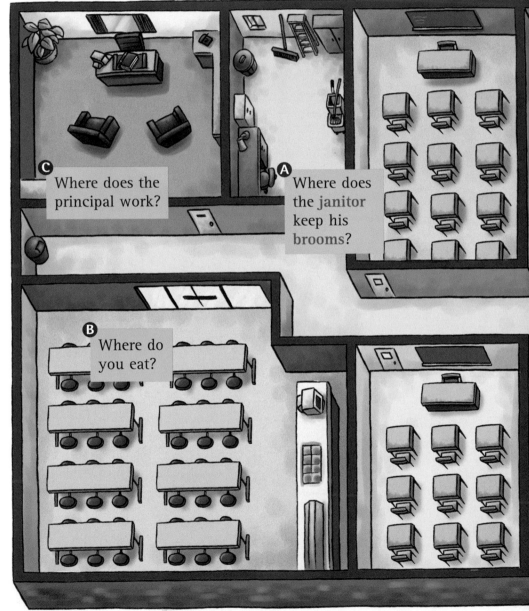

C Where does the principal work?

A Where does the janitor keep his brooms?

B Where do you eat?

word bank

- locker room
- English class
- cafeteria
- supply room
- principal's office

■ Hint #4

If you get in trouble, you will be very close.

■ Hint #5

You will find the book on a large desk.

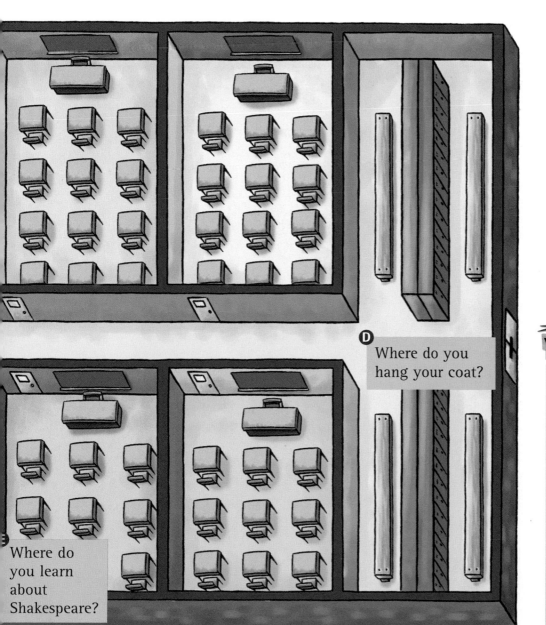

D Where do you hang your coat?

Where do you learn about Shakespeare?

vocabulary

broom:

far away: at a great distance.

hint: a clue, helpful information.

janitor: a person who cleans and takes care of the school.

supply room: a room used to store paper, products, janitor's equipment.

Old School, New School

Activity 2

Do you miss your old school? Do you prefer your new school?

1. **Look at** the pictures.

2. **Listen to** the four students talk about schools.

3. **Find** out who is talking.

4. What do these students miss? What do they prefer now?

5. What do you miss? What do you prefer now? See **Talk About It.**

TALK ABOUT IT!

A) Alexander

C) Rebecca

B) Audrey

D) Max

Preferences

I miss...		I prefer...	
	my friends.		my new school building.
	my teachers.		my new friends.
	my old schoolyard.		my new teachers.
	etc.		my schedule.
			etc.

School Activities... They're Extra!

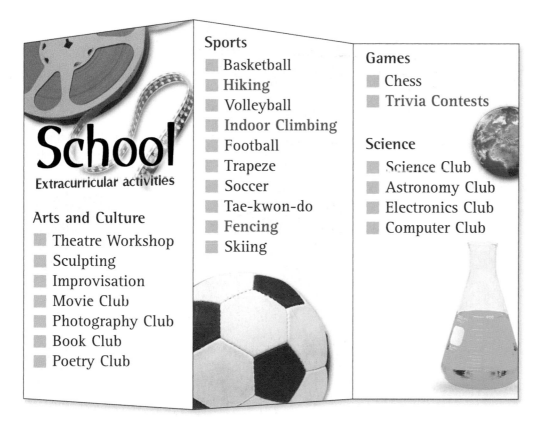

School
Extracurricular activities

Arts and Culture
- [ ] Theatre Workshop
- [ ] Sculpting
- [ ] Improvisation
- [ ] Movie Club
- [ ] Photography Club
- [ ] Book Club
- [ ] Poetry Club

Sports
- [ ] Basketball
- [ ] Hiking
- [ ] Volleyball
- [ ] Indoor Climbing
- [ ] Football
- [ ] Trapeze
- [ ] Soccer
- [ ] Tae-kwon-do
- [ ] Fencing
- [ ] Skiing

Games
- [ ] Chess
- [ ] Trivia Contests

Science
- [ ] Science Club
- [ ] Astronomy Club
- [ ] Electronics Club
- [ ] Computer Club

STEP 1

Is school only about learning in class? Do you practice any extracurricular activities at lunchtime or after school?

Before Reading

1. **Scan** the activity pamphlet.

2. How many kinds of activities are listed?

Reading

3. **Choose** five activities that you would like to do.

4. **Write down** the name of your five activities.

After reading

5. Which activities are offered in your school?

6. Where else can you participate in these activities?

▼ | **Reinvest**

7. Ask five classmates about their five favourite activities.

8. **Write down** the name of their favourite activities.

9. Which activities are the most popular? **Draw a graph** to show your results.

vo**c**A**b**u**l**a**r**y

fencing:

hiking:

indoor climbing:

trivia contest: a quiz game.

Sense or Non-sense Classroom Rules

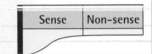

STEP 2

Does your class have a lot of rules? Do they all make sense?

Before reading

1. **Skim rules** A to O. Did you find a non-sense rule?

2. **Draw** two columns; one for sense and one for non-sense.

Sense	Non-sense

STRATEGY

See **Skim**, p. 192.

A) Don't chew gum in class.

B) Raise your foot to ask a question.

C) No pets are allowed in class, not even tigers.

D) You may not bring your lunch to class.

E) Hand in your work on time.

F) Be punctual.

G) It is permitted to use punctuation in class.

H) It is forbidden to brush your teeth in class.

WRITE ABOUT IT!

Instructions

To give instructions, use verbs in the **imperative form.**

- To tell someone **to do** something, begin your sentence with the *verb*.

  Examples: **Put your hat on,** it's cold outside.
  Write your name and group number on the sheet.

- To tell someone **not to do** something, begin your sentence with *Don't + verb.*

  Examples: **Don't chew** gum in class.
  Don't tell me you forgot your homework.

I) You must ask permission to get up and walk around.

J) When the bell rings, do not answer the door or the telephone.

K) Respect yourself, your classmates and your teacher.

L) Don't litter the classroom.

M) Don't use your X-ray vision to see the answers in the teacher's guide.

N) Using cake icing as ink is prohibited when writing texts.

O) Glasses must be worn on the nose at all times.

Reading

3. As you read, **write down** the rule in the correct column (sense or non-sense). ✏️

After reading

4. Which rules do you think would work in your class?

5. Which rules do you already follow?

▼ Reinvest

6. Write down two of your class rules. One rule that permits something, and one that forbids something. See **Write About It**. ✏️

VOCABULARY

forbidden: not permitted.

to litter:

prohibited: not permitted.

rule: a statement that indicates what is permitted and what is forbidden.

What did you learn in school today?

Not enough. I have to go back tomorrow!

The Uncanny Teachers

This is the story about my first day in secondary school.

STEP 3

All teachers are unique. Wait until you hear about Rudy's teachers.

Before listening

1. **Look at** the comic strip.

2. Are the frames of the comic strip in the correct order?

3. On your handout, **write down** the letter of the frames and the time in the correct order.

Listening

4. **Listen to** Rudy's first day at school.

5. On your handout, **write down** the letter of the rooms and the **subjects**.

Welcome to computer class

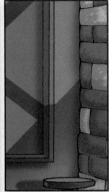

What would you get if you crossed a vampire and a teacher?

Lots of blood tests!

STRATEGY

See **Infer with visual clues,** p. 191.

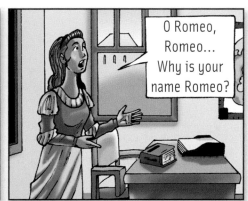

VOCABULARY

subject: course, *examples:* Math, English, Science, History, etc.

uncanny: strange or particular.

▼ **Reinvest**

8. On your handout, **draw** a timeline of the school day.

9. **Write down** the **subjects**, times and room numbers in the school day.

Schools Around the World

STEP 4 📄

Do you think your school is a good school? Do you have everything you need to learn? Are you working too hard? These are letters from teens your age who live around the world.

Before Reading

1. **Scan** the letters to find where these teens come from.

2. **Name** the countries you know and their continent.

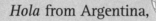

Asia	North America
Africa	South America
	Europe

Reading

3. **Read** the letters.

4. On the handout, **fill in** the table with the information you find.

Keiko, 13

Konnichiwa from Japan,

I wear a uniform and all my classes have 40 students. After lunch, each class is assigned to an area of the school for *osoji*, which means to clean up. Soon, I will start *juku*, an afternoon school to prepare for my university entrance.

Hola from Argentina,

I go to school only in the morning. After lunch, I go to work to help my family. Next year I will quit school to work full-time because we need the money. I will finish my secondary studies when I'm about 21.

Jacinto, 13

Hej from Sweden,

I live in Gothenburg near the Norwegian border. Education is very important here and until I **pursue** university studies, my parents don't have to pay anything; not even my food when I'm in school. I spend 8 hours per day in my *grundskola*.

Erik, 14

STRATEGY

See **Scan,** p. 192.

TALK ABOUT IT!

Opinions

I **think...**	...my school has good teachers.
I **believe...**	...we are luckier than teens in Afghanistan.
In my opinion, ...	...Japanese schools are too strict.
From my point of view, ...	...Russian teens and schools need more money.

Abir, 12

Raisa, 14

After Reading

5. Would you like to **switch places** with one of these students? Which one?

6. Do you like your school the way it is?

Salaam from Afghanistan,

A few years ago, I was not permitted to go to school because I am a girl. War has been very hard on my country and our schools are in very bad shape. I have to share my textbooks and we sit on the floor.

Privet from Russia,

School here used to be free for everyone but economic problems are forcing things to change. We can now read all kinds of books because they're not banned anymore and politics are no longer part of our courses. We have classes like you do.

VOCABULARY

banned: not permitted.

border: frontier.

to pursue: to continue.

to switch places: to exchange places, to trade places.

Maalik, 12

Hello from Zambia,

I'm not in school this year. My family has no money to send me. This year I will hunt and fish. My sister goes to school because the government wants more girls in schools. All classes are in English because we were a British colony.

CULTURE

English as a first or second language is spoken in over 80 countries by about 875 million people. Some people estimate that a similar number of people are learning English as a foreign language. That's over 1,600,000,000 people!

▼ **Reinvest**

7. Do you think school is important?

8. What is different between your school and these teens' schools? See **Talk About It.**

Whiz Quiz Tips

Project A
Getting Started

Do you like to show off your knowledge in a good quiz game? Do you know how to plan a quiz?

Before Reading

1. **Skim** the page to get a general idea what the text is about.

2. What is the **topic** in the text?
   • game rules;
   • **tips** to create a game;
   • the story of a game.

Reading

3. **Read** the text.

After reading

4. Do this information can help you create a quiz?

5. Do you have enough information to start producing your game?

■ **Don't forget!**
A quiz game must be simple in order to be fun.

A) Use simple rules to play. Write them down so the **contestants** learn them before playing.

B) Create a game that can be played with a **whole** group or with three or four players.

C) Designate a game master. The game master asks the questions, calculates the points and crowns the winner.

D) Write down clear, simple and precise questions. A **contestant** must be able to respond quickly if he or she knows the answer.

An ideal homework excuse

Where is your homework?

I lost it having a quarrel with this kid who said you weren't the best teacher in the school.

"How to" guide.
Here are a few suggestions for producing a basic quiz game.

E) Make cue cards on which to write your questions and answers.

F) A quiz game doesn't require a board, so don't make one.

G) Use colours for different question categories.
Example:

SPORTS   ARTS   LANGUAGE   SCHOOL

H) Give one point for good answers, nothing for bad answers.

I) Start with one round and eliminate the contestants with the least points. Then start again with the remaining players until you have only one player left who will be your winner.

Example:

If you have eight players or teams:

Round 1: everyone plays.   👤👤👤👤👤👤👤👤

Round 2: 4 players or teams play.   👤👤👤👤

Round 3: 2 players or teams play.   👤👤

Then you get your winner(s).   (👤)

J) You have to write about 24 question cards.

▼ **Reinvest**

The School Quiz   **PROJECT A**

Using the template provided by your teacher, create a quiz game about your school and general culture with different categories in it.

In your questions, include the new words you learned about both your school environment and your classmates.

Voc**A**b**u**L**a**r**y**

contestant: player.

cue card:

SPORTS

tip: suggestion.

topic: the subject of a text, a book, a discussion, etc.

whole: complete, entire.

The Art of Scheduling

Project B
Getting Started

Do you like your schedule? Do you think you start too early in the morning? Or finish too late in the afternoon?

Before reading

1. **Look at** these three schedules.

2. What kind of information do you find in a schedule?

Reading

3. As you read, **pay attention** to the details in each schedule.
   - Classes per day;
   - Duration of the classes;
   - Duration of the lunch break;
   - Time the school day starts and ends.

4. On your handout, **compare** these schedules by filling in the table.

STRATEGY

See **Compare,** p. 188.

Schedule A

	MONDAY	TUESDAY	WEDNESDAY
7:30 a.m. to 8:30 a.m.	Math Room 110	French Room 115	English Room 105
8:40 a.m. to 9:40 a.m.	History Room 120	Gym Room 005	Art Room 300
9:50 a.m. to 10:50 a.m.	French Room 115	Science Room 100	Science Room 100
11:00 a.m. to 12:00 a.m.	Science Room 100	Math Room 110	French Room 115
12:00 a.m. to 12:50 p.m.	Lunch	Lunch	Lunch
12:50 p.m. to 1:50 p.m.	Art Room 300	English Room 105	History Room 120
2:00 p.m. to 3:00 p.m.	Music Room 325	History Room 120	Math Room 110

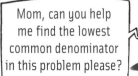

Mom, can you help me find the lowest common denominator in this problem please?

Don't tell me they haven't found it yet; I remember looking for it when I was a girl!

Schedule B

	8:30 a.m. 10:30 a.m.	10:40 a.m. 12:40 p.m.	12:40 p.m. 2:00 p.m.	2:10 p.m. 4:10 p.m.
Monday	Art Room B-20	French Room A-10	Lunch	Science Room C-15
Tuesday	French Room A-10	English Room A-25	Lunch	History Room C-10
Wednesday	Gym Room D-10	Math Room A-40	Lunch	French Room A-10

After reading

5. Which of these schedules do you prefer?

6. Which one is the easiest to read?

7. How is your own schedule?

Schedule C

	Monday	Tuesday	Wednesday
9:30 a.m. to 10:45 a.m.	French Room 100	Art Room 029	English Room 125
10:55 a.m. to 12:10 p.m.	History Room 315	Math Room 324	Gym Room 001
12:10 p.m. to 1:25 p.m.	Lunch	Lunch	Lunch
1:30 p.m. to 2:45 p.m.	Math Room 324	English Room 125	Science Room 013
2:55 p.m. to 4:10 p.m.	Science Room 013	French Room 100	History Room 315

▼ Reinvest

Your Dream Schedule   PROJECT B

How about creating your own schedule that would fit your own needs?

In your project, don't forget to include details such as:
- duration of classes;
- room numbers;
- name of subjects or activities;
- distance between rooms;
- the hour you would like to start and end;
- etc.

High School Woes

Project C
Getting Started

PART 1

Did you have any problems adapting to your new school? Was it hard to make new friends?

Before Reading

1. **Look at** the texts.

2. **What type** of texts are these?

3. **To whom** are they sent?

Reading

4. **Read** the texts.

5. **Write down** the problems each student faces.

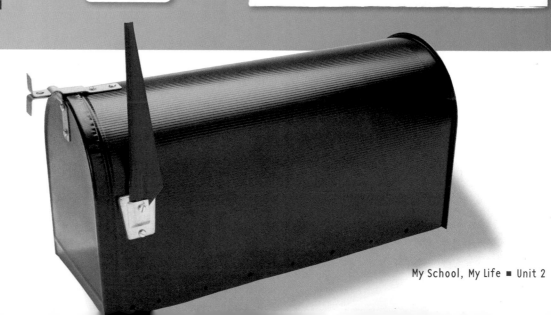

Letter A

Dear Dr. S. Cool,

I hate my uniform!!!
It's blue, green and white, all colours that I don't like. My mom says it makes me look neat! I don't want to look neat! What will girls think of me in that suit?

Young rebel

Letter B

To: drscool@epalmail.kick
From: lostgirl@epalmail.kick
Subject: can't find my way...

Dear Dr. S. Cool,

My new school is so huge. I can't find my way to my classes. It takes me forever to get to my next class. They're too far apart! My school has too many wings, hallways and doors. How can I find my way in this labyrinth?

Lost girl

Letter C

Dear Dr. S. Cool,

I have a gigantic problem! My backpack is my gigantic trouble. At the end of the day it's so full that it's heavier than me! My back hurts. I don't know what to do because I need my books and binders and all my school supplies for my classes.

Biting off more than I can chew

To: drscool@epalmail.kick
From: fishoutofwater@epalmail.kick
Subject: daydreaming

Hello Dr. S. Cool,

I have problems concentrating and I can't sleep. I make tons of mistakes and I'm always **daydreaming**. My friends tell me that I have my **head in the clouds**. I never know when classes start or end. I can't find my books and I'm always late.

Fish out of water

Letter D

After Reading

6. What can you tell them in order to help them?

7. What was the first problem you had when you arrived in your new school?

VOCABULARY

daydreaming: head in the clouds:

hallway: corridor.

huge: very large.

neat: clean, in order.

wing: section.

woes: problems, troubles.

IDIOM

to bite off more than *you* can chew:

to try to do more than you can do.

to be like a fish out of water:

to feel out of place, to be in the wrong place.

Dr. S. Cool's Do's and Don'ts

Here are Dr. S. Cool's solution to your problems.

Project C
Getting Started

PART 2

Reading

1. **Read** Dr. S. Cool's solutions.

2. **Match** these solutions with the letters on pages 36 and 37.

After reading

3. Do you think the doctor gives good advice?

4. Would you try it?

vOCABulary

to fuss: to worry, to create unnecessary problems.

to lie: to tell something that is untrue.

to plan ahead: to think about something in advance.

to tag along: to follow someone.

truthful: sincere.

Do's

1. Use your agenda; it's the key to punctuality. Use the school map in your agenda. Mark your classrooms with a colour code. You will never be late again!

2. Be yourself and you will make friends fast.

3. Use your locker. It will keep all your things safe while you're in class. Exchange your books during your breaks.

4. Write down everything you need to do at home (homework, studying, projects) to plan your evenings ahead. Planning = relaxing.

5. When you feel like you're in a difficult situation, ask an adult from your school to help you.

Don'ts

6. Don't act like a parasite with other students. It's all right to ask for help and tag along, but make sure you learn what they show you.

7. Don't fuss over school rules. Do what you have to do and at the end of the day, you will be free to go home.

8. Don't lie to your teachers. Eventually, they will find you out and you will always feel you're being watched. Be truthful, even when you are in trouble.

9. Don't worry about your uniform or your looks. Everybody at your school is wearing one.

▼ Reinvest

A Secondary Cycle One Survival Guide   PROJECT C

It's important to share your experience and knowledge about your new school with future Secondary Cycle One students.

Don't forget to include in your project:

- problems and solutions experienced by your classmates;
- comic strips, photos or illustrations to make your guide fun to read;
- a clear and precise "do's and don'ts" list.

Your Project Presentation

- Did you work individually or in teams?
- Was each task you had to do clear?
- How much time did you spend on your project?
- Do you need more time to rehearse in order to prepare for your presentation or to do your school quiz?
- Do you have all the material you need for the presentation?
- Which part of your presentation do you think your classmates will prefer?

- Is there any part of your project that you need to double-check with your teacher?

It's time to present your project.

Take risks, speak clearly and focus on the most important facts so your presentation will be interesting.

Your Portfolio

During this unit, you experienced a lot of different activities related to school life and your environment. You learned to use some new words and expressions; you learned to use new strategies when interacting orally, or reading and listening to texts.

Be sure to put the following items in your portfolio:

- The *In this Unit* handout, to self-evaluate your learning in relation to oral interactions, texts and strategies.
- All the notes and short texts you wrote in the Reinvest section at the end of some of the activities.
- The *Vocabulary* and *Language* handouts that you completed.
- The *Evaluation* handouts you completed.
- Any texts, documents, pictures or handouts you used during your project.

Scary Stories

1. Look at the monster gallery.
2. A monster's portrait is missing on the wall.
3. Read the description of the missing monster.
4. Draw the monster on a sheet of paper.

MISSING MONSTER DESCRIPTION

THIS MONSTER HAS THREE EYES: ONE GREEN, ONE GREY AND ONE RED.

IT HAS SIX ARMS AND LONG CLAWS ON ITS PAWS.

IT HAS CROCODILE SKIN AND A BLACK TWISTED TAIL.

ITS HAIR IS PURPLE AND LOOKS LIKE SNAKES.

ITS TEETH ARE YELLOW AND ITS LIPS ARE DARK BLUE.

THIS MONSTER LOOKS FURIOUS.

IN THIS UNIT

You Will...

- talk about and describe Halloween costumes and scary characters;

- read and discover some scary stories and their key elements;

- listen to and identify scary sounds;

- vote for your favourite scary movies.

Text Types

Look at, read and/or listen to...

riddles, legends, comic strips, a biography, short stories, movie reviews, a survey, a magazine article.

Key elements of short stories: characters, setting, storyline.

Strategies

- predict with pictures;
- compare;
- scan.

Projects

Write or produce one of the following projects:

- *A Scary Story Review;*
- *Halloween Costume Parade;*
- *A Frightening Skit.*

Favourite Halloween Costumes

VOCABULARY

crooked nose:
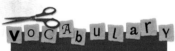

stitches:
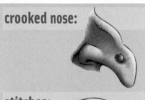

A) My costume represents a small legendary human-like creature.

B) I have a long **crooked nose** and a pointed hat. I hold a broom.

C) I am covered with a big white sheet. All you can see are my eyes.

D) I look like a cat. I am strong and mysterious.

E) My face is horrible. I have **stitches** on my forehead. My skin is green.

F) I wear red and there are horns on my head. I carry a fork. I'm bad.

u m e s

5   6   7   8

Why was 9 scared of 7?

Because 7 8 9.

CULTURE

In her famous novel, entitled *Frankenstein*, Mary Shelley recounts the story of a scientist. He wants to create a better human. Instead, he produces a monster. The novel was published in 1818. It has inspired many movies and books.

Character Description

My favourite costume is...   colour (red, black, blue, etc.)

My character wears...   name of clothes (a suit, a coat, a hat, etc.)

It is a...   type of character (dwarf, ghost, pirate, etc.)

TALK ABOUT IT!

Halloween Sounds

Activity 2

How do you react to strange sounds? Do they scare you?

1. **Look at** the illustrations of scary sounds.

2. **Imagine** which sounds might match the illustrations.

3. **Listen to** the scary sounds.

4. **Match** the descriptions to the pictures.

5. **How** do you feel when you hear these sounds? See **Talk About It.**

STRATEGY

See **Predict** with pictures, p. 187.

④

Feelings

I feel ...
  anxious .
  scared .
  nervous .
  worried .
  frightened .
  calm .

⑤

TALK ABOUT IT!

VOCABULARY

howling: the loud cry of a dog or wolf, especially when in pain.

⑥

⑦

■ **Descriptions:**

A) The witch is laughing.

B) The moon is full. The wolves are howling.

C) Poor cat! Why is it screaming?

D) Can you hear the ghost lamenting?

E) I'm scared of stormy nights. I hate the sound of thunder.

F) Can you hear the wind blowing?

G) The door is banging.

Why didn't the skeleton go to the party?

Because he had no body to go with.

A Halloween Legend

Once upon a time, there lived a miserable old man. He was called Stingy Jack. He liked to play tricks on people and was a very bad person. When he died, he was condemned to haunt the Earth by night.

But Stingy Jack was very scared of the dark. How was he going to find his way? He could not see. Stingy Jack took a **turnip** from his pocket. He always had turnips in his pockets because he liked to eat them. Jack **carved** a hole in the turnip. He placed a hot coal inside it. This way he could see.

Since that day, Stingy Jack has walked the Earth. He has no place to rest. He lights his way with his turnip lantern. People who thought they saw him, called him Jack of the Lantern, and later *Jack-o'-lantern.*

On Halloween night, Irish people traditionally carve turnips, potatoes, beets and other vegetables. They place a light inside. These lanterns scare Stingy Jack and other bad spirits away.

STEP 1

Do you know that carved pumpkins are called jack-o'-lanterns? Jack-o'-lanterns come from an old Irish legend.

Before Reading

1. Do you like legends?

2. What is a legend?
   - a true story;
   - fiction;
   - an old, partly true story.

Reading

3. **Read** the text.

4. What is the character's name?

5. What name do people give the character at the end of the story?

to carve: to cut or shape something.

stingy: ungenerous.

turnip:

C U L T U R E

When Irish immigrants came to North America, they discovered pumpkins. They are bigger and easier to carve than turnips or potatoes. Today, we still use pumpkins and call them jack-o'-lanterns.

Key Elements of a Text

The following **key elements** sum up the most important facts in a literary text:

The **setting**: when and where the action happens;
The **characters**: who are responsible for the story action;
The **storyline**: what happens during the story.

Example:

Nightmare of the Living Dead

On a dark Halloween night, three careless teenagers decide to take a walk in the cemetery. They find several open graves and empty coffins. Frightened, they run away and hear the footsteps of a monstrous zombie following them. One of the teenagers falls down. The two others hide behind a tombstone. They hear the horrible screams of their friend. One of the teens shakes the shoulders of the other saying, "Wake up Ben! Wake up! It's just a nightmare!"

The **setting**: in a cemetery on a dark Halloween night.

The **characters**: three careless teenagers; a monstrous zombie.

The **storyline**:

■ They decide to walk. ■ They hear the zombie and they run. ■ They hear their friend's screams. ■ They wake up.

TALK ABOUT IT!

▼ Reinvest

8. Can you retell the story?

9. Put this storyline in order. See **Talk About It**.

■ Stingy Jack turns a turnip into a lantern. ■ People call Jack, "Jack-o'-lantern" ■ Stingy Jack is a bad man who dies.

After reading

6. The Jack-o'-lantern legend explains...
   • ...why there are ghosts;
   • ...the origin of the carved pumpkin;
   • ...Stingy Jack's new name.

7. Did you like the story?

VOCABULARY

coffin:

grave: an excavation in the ground to bury a dead body.

nightmare: a bad dream.

tombstone:

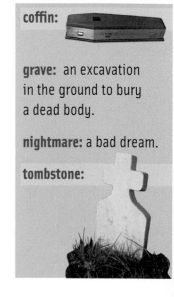

Our Dinner With Dracula

STEP 2

PART 1

Do you know any Dracula stories? Do you think you know everything about Dracula? Does Dracula really exist?

Before Reading

1. **Look at** the pictures.

2. What type of text is it?
   • a short story;
   • an article;
   • a biography.

Reading

3. **Read** the text.

STRATEGY

See **Predict**, p. 187.

What did the lady tell Dracula?

Sometimes you're a real pain in the neck.

It was a windy evening. Both Martha and I could feel a storm coming. So before it started to rain, we stopped at a French bistro. We ordered our favourite dish, *escargots à l'ail.*

Someone in the restaurant was staring at Martha. I turned around and saw a distinguished gentleman. He had dark black hair. His eyes were like dark coals. He had a mustache and his fingernails were very long. He was wearing a tuxedo, a cape with a high collar and a top hat. He was strange.

4. In this text, is Dracula an historical character or an imaginary character?

After Reading

5. In which paragraph is the setting of the story presented?

The gentleman joined us at the table. He had just arrived from Romania. His name was Vlad. He was visiting **relatives**. We talked about music, books, movies and many other things. It was like talking to an old friend. The storm finally broke. We could see lightning in the sky and hear the thunder. Martha and I were scared. We hate storms.

garlic:

relatives: other family members.

smell: odour.

to stare: to look long and hard.

Vlad sat closer... and he tried to kiss Martha, but the **smell** of **garlic** and that made him uncomfortable. Then suddenly Vlad disappeared just as a bat flew over my head.

CULTURE

Gothic literature is a British tradition. The best examples of this form of literature are Mary Shelley's *Frankenstein* and Bram Stoker's *Dracula*.

Edgar Allan Poe's short stories revived this tradition in America.

PART 2

Before reading

7. Skim over the text by reading the subtitles.

8. What will you discover about Dracula?

9. What type of text is it?
- a short story;
- an article;
- a biography.

Reading

10. Read the text *The Truth About Dracula.*

11. What does the name "Dracula" mean?

After Reading

12. In this text, is Dracula an historical character or only an imaginary character?

13. Which text did you prefer between *Our Dinner with Dracula* (p.48-49) and *The Truth About Dracula* (this page)?

The Truth About Dracula

The Son of the Dragon

Dracula was born in Transylvania (Romania) in 1431. He was a prince and a soldier. With his father Dracul* and his brother Mircea, he was a member of the Order of the Dragon. His father and brother were imprisoned by their enemies and died.

Vlad Tepes

Dracula's real name was Vlad Tepes. In Romanian, Tepes means *impaler*. Prince Vlad was very cruel and violent. He used terror to scare his enemies. He died in 1476, near Bucharest, Romania. He was buried in a monastery on the island of Snagov.

The Ghost of Dracula

In 1931, archaeologists discovered a grave in Snagov. There was a skeleton inside the casket. The skeleton was wearing clothes similar to Dracula's. He was wearing a long cape. On his head, he had a crown with turquoise stones. He was wearing a ring with the emblem of the Order of the Dragon.

The archaeologists sent these findings to a museum in Bucharest. Since then, everything has disappeared. No one knows what happened. It's a mystery. This was the beginning of the legend of Dracula.

Many people still wonder if the legend of Dracula is really fact or fantasy.

* In Romanian, Dracul means *dragon*.

STRATEGY

See **Compare**, p. 188.

▼ Reinvest

14. On your handout, **compare** the texts *The Truth About Dracula* and *Our Dinner with Dracula.*

Scary Movies Awards

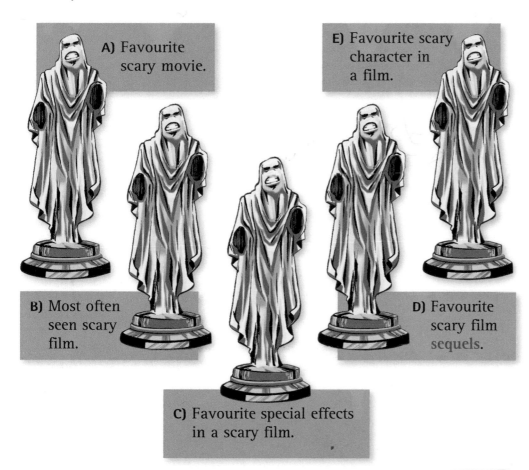

A) Favourite scary movie.

E) Favourite scary character in a film.

B) Most often seen scary film.

D) Favourite scary film sequels.

C) Favourite special effects in a scary film.

STEP 3

Do you like horror, fantasy or science fiction films? Do you prefer to watch movies at home or at the theatre?

Before Reading

1. **Name** as many scary movie titles as you know.

Reading

2. **Read** the five **award** categories.

3. **Ask** your classmates questions about the **award** categories. See **Talk About It**.

4. **Write down** the names of the nominees.

After Reading

5. Which questions were the most difficult to answer?

Questions with What

question word   +   verb   +   subject.

Example:

| What | is | your favorite scary movie? |
| | | the scary film you have seen most often? |

TALK ABOUT IT!

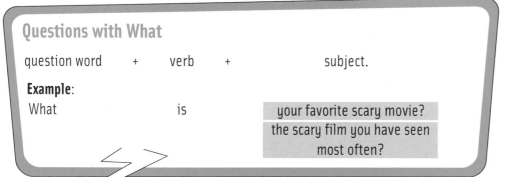

▼ Reinvest

6. Share your answers with your classmates.

7. Choose three nominees for each category.

8. Vote for each **award**.

award:

casket:

sequel: a movie that continues where an earlier movie ended.

to wonder: to want to know.

Project A
Getting Started

Do you read movie or book reviews on Web sites?

Before reading

1. **Scan** the text to find the **ratings**.

2. **Take a look** at the titles on the posters.

Reading

3. **Read** the movie reviews.

4. **Match** each review to the appropriate poster.

STRATEGY

See **Scan**, p. 192.

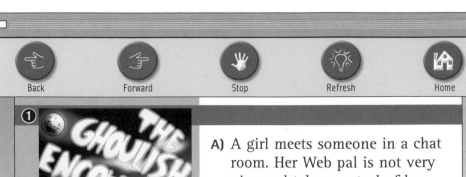

Back　　Forward　　Stop　　Refresh　　Home

①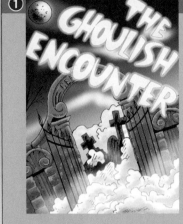

A) A girl meets someone in a chat room. Her Web pal is not very nice and takes control of her computer. Fortunately, her mother turns off the switch.

Good thriller, a real nail biter!

②

B) There's a strange new teacher at school. When given a **detention**, Edith finds out that the teacher is really a werewolf.

Boring! Do you really want to see this one?

▼ **Reinvest**

A Scary Story Review

PROJECT A

Do you sometimes ask your friends or classmates for their comments about a new movie or story? Do you like to give your own comments?

In this project, you will review a scary movie or a scary story. Include a short description of the setting and the main characters. Then give a rating (one to five) and a short comment.

③

C) On a dark cold Halloween night, a man's car breaks down; he's at a crossroads in front of a cemetery. Suddenly, a creepy ghoul confronts him.

Weird, the storyline is confusing.

④

D) The Smith family has just moved into their new house. The eldest son starts behaving strangely. A poltergeist has taken over his room.

Predictable, but it has good moments.

After reading

5. Which of these movies has the best review? Which has the worst?

6. Which movie would you like to watch?

What did one skeleton say to the other skeleton?

It's going to rain. I can feel it in my bones!

VoCabulary

detention: when you are kept in the classroom after school.

ghoul: an evil spirit.

poltergeist: a noisy ghost.

rating: evaluation.

Your Favourite Halloween Costume

Project B
Getting Started

Do you like to dress up for Halloween night? Maybe you can get some ideas here.

Before Reading

1. **Look at** the pictures.

2. Can you name the different monsters?

3. Which is your favourite?

Reading

4. **Read** the descriptions of the costumes.

5. In your notebook, **draw** a table like this one. ◖▮▮◖━━▶

Character's name	Clothes	Colours	Special features

My name is William. I'm dressed up as a skeleton. I am wearing a tight, black costume. There are white bones painted on my costume. I have no hair. I am wearing a white mask.

1

2

My name is Karina. I'm dressed up as a ghoul. I'm also dressed in black. I'm wearing black gloves. I have only two fingers. I have horns on my forehead. I have two enormous ears. I have a large mouth with long, sharp teeth.

3

My name is Edward. I'm dressed up as the Grim Reaper. I'm wearing a large, loose, black robe. It has a **huge hood**. It is pulled over my face. I'm holding a **huge**, long axe.

vocabulary

feature: an important characteristic.

hood: part of a cloak that covers the head.

huge: big, very large.

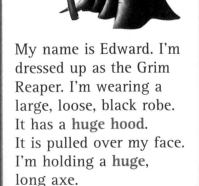

4

My name is Samia. I'm dressed up as a mummy. I'm wearing bandages all over my body. The bandages are dirty and torn.

5

My name is Jordan. I'm dressed as a werewolf. I'm wearing old clothes. I have hair on my face and on my hands. I have long, pointed ears. I have big hands with very long nails. My teeth are very sharp.

6

My name is Quyn. I'm dressed up as a zombie. I'm wearing old clothes. They are falling apart. My face is dirty. I walk with my hands straight in front of me. My eyes are dead. I smell horrible.

Reading

6. **Fill in** your table with specific information about the characters.

After Reading

7. **Compare** the information you put in the table with a classmate.

8. **Make a list** of all the adjectives you find in the text.

What did the man say after the vampire bit him?

"He got the best out of me."

▼ **Reinvest**

Halloween Costume Parade   **PROJECT B**

Do you celebrate Halloween at school? With your classmates? Have you ever participated in a costume parade?

What makes a costume parade fun is the descriptions of the costumes. In your description, include the name of the character, the names and colours of the clothes in the costume and any adjectives or special features you need to describe your character.

Project C
Getting Started

What makes you scared? Do you believe in were-wolves?

Before Reading

1. **Look at** the comic strip.

2. What is the setting of the story?

3. How many characters are there in the story?

Reading

4. **Read** the dialogues.

After reading

5. **Team up** with two classmates.

6. **Choose** a character and imagine his or her voice.

7. With your classmates, **act out** the story.

8. What does "To be continued" mean?

> Kevin, I need your help. I am in real trouble. I'm in the cemetery near...

Click

> What do we do? This is dangerous.

> We have no choice. What if Vivi gets hurt? We have to find her.

> I have a bad feeling about this.

> Oh, please relax Ginny! Let's be brave.

> Wait! Something is not right.

> Look! Vivianne is safe.

> Don't come. There's something in the bushes.

> What is it? What's wrong?

> Don't worry Vivi, we're here. We will help you.

To be continued

 Reinvest

 A Frightening Skit   **PROJECT C**

Choose one of these endings for the story or **invent** an ending of your own.

1. It is a werewolf. It is lonely and looking for friends.
2. It is a trick. Vivi wants to play a trick on her friends.
3. The werewolf is frightened by the sound of sirens. He runs away.

Your Project Presentation

- • Was your teamwork effective?
- Did everyone on the team complete his/her tasks?
- Was each task you had to do clear?
- How much time did you spend on your project?
- Do you need more practice to prepare for your presentation?
- Do you have all the material you need for the presentation?
- Do you feel what you have prepared will captivate the audience?

It's time to present your project.

Take your time, speak clearly and focus on your pronunciation and intonation so everyone will understand you.

Your Portfolio

In this unit, you experienced a lot of different activities related to Halloween, monsters and costumes, scary stories and movies. You learned to use some new words and expressions, you also learned to use new strategies when interacting orally, reading and listening to texts.

Be sure to put the following items in your portfolio:

- The *In this Unit* handout, to self-evaluate your learning in relation to oral interactions, texts and strategies.
- All the notes and short texts you wrote in the Reinvest section at the end of some of the activities.
- The *Vocabulary* and *Language* handouts that you completed.
- The *Evaluation* handouts you completed.
- Any texts, documents, pictures or handouts you used during your project.

Ⓑ compilation
knock out

Ⓐ alone in the mass
THE LONERS

Have you ever tried to find a CD without knowing the title or the artist?
What's another way of finding a CD?

C *meadow*
daisy dandelion

D ROW AWAY
The Sailors

E can you
see the
LIGHT

F DON"T SHOW
ME YOURS
FINGERS

1. Look at the CD inserts on pages 58 and 59.
2. Listen to the dialogue.
3. Find the CDs they're talking about.

IN THIS UNIT
You Will...

- talk about your musical tastes and listening habits;

- listen to selections of different styles of music;

- read about and discuss topics including the media, fashion, technology, music history, special artists and musicians, etc.

Text Types

Look at, read and/or listen to...

labels, timelines, comic strips, biographies, questionnaires, music excerpts, advertisements (poster, flyer, etc.), song lyrics, encyclopedia and magazine articles.

Key elements of songs: verse, chorus, rhyme.

Strategies

- take notes;
- compare;
- infer with cognates and contextual cues;
- scan.

Projects

Write or produce one of the following projects:

- *An Artist's Timeline;*
- *A Musical Survey;*
- *The Radio Show;*
- *Promote Your Own Show.*

Test Your Musical Knowledge

Activity 1

Do you know much about music and musical culture? Try this little test; you still might learn a thing or two.

1. **Read** the questions.

2. **Answer** them in your notebook. ✏️

3. **Check** your answers with your teacher.

4. How many questions did you get right?

A) Who holds the record for the most #1 hits?
- Elton John
- Elvis Presley
- The Beatles

B) What city does "Grunge rock" come from?
- New York
- Detroit
- Seattle
- Boston

C) Put the following recording devices in chronological order starting with the oldest.
- compact disc
- 33 1/3-rpm records
- metal cylinder
- cassette tape

D) What musical instrument is played more than any other by teenagers today?
- drums
- piano
- electric guitar
- acoustic guitar

E) How many strings does an electric lead guitar have?
- 4
- 6
- 8
- 10

F) To what family of musical instruments does the flute belong?
- brass
- percussion
- woodwind
- strings

G) Which composer's life is highlighted in the movie *Amadeus*?
- Bach
- Beethoven
- Mozart
- Verdi
- Haydn

H) Put the following musical styles in chronological order starting with the oldest.
- punk rock
- blues
- hip hop
- swing
- disco

I) Where did John Lennon and Yoko Ono sing *Give Peace a Chance* for the first time?
- Boston
- Washington
- Montreal
- Paris
- Toronto

J) Which female artist has sold the most albums in her career?
- Britney Spears
- Céline Dion
- Diana Ross
- Avril Lavigne

hit: a great success.

string: a thin cord or wire.

Your Musical Habits

A) Do you like to sing?
- ■ Yes, I sing in the shower.
- ■ Yes, I sing in the car.
- ■ Yes, I sing in a choir.
- ■ No, I don't.

B) What do you use to listen to music?
- ■ I use my MP3 player.
- ■ I listen to music on my radio in my room.
- ■ I pump up the volume of the car's sound system.

C) When do you listen to music?
- ■ In the morning while I prepare for school.
- ■ On my lunch break.
- ■ After school, before I do my homework.

D) Where do you listen to music?
- ■ In my room.
- ■ On the school bus.
- ■ In the basement of my house.

E) Why do you listen to music?
- ■ Because I can relax.
- ■ Because it makes me feel good.
- ■ Because when I walk home, the time goes faster.

F) Who do you listen to music with?
- ■ With my friends.
- ■ Alone.

Activity 2

When do you listen to music? Do you have a favourite place where you can go and relax?

1. **Read** the questions and the choice of answers.

2. **Answer** each question by yourself.

3. Then **ask** the questions to a partner.

4. **Compare** your answers.

choir: a group of singers.

to pump up: to turn the volume up.

Music and Emotions

Activity 3

Music always makes you feel something. Whatever your state, you can always find music that will **fit you like a glove**.

1. **Listen to** five short musical selections.

2. On your handout, **note** your emotions or state, the musical style and one instrument or sound you hear in each selection.

Emotions – States

humorous – funny

frightened – scared

sad – moody

energized

aggressive

romantic

calm – relaxed

Idiom

to fit like a glove: to be exactly right, just what you need.

Instruments – Sounds

WINDS

trumpet

woodwinds

STRINGS

acoustic guitar

violin

grand piano

BELLOWS-TYPE INSTRUMENTS

harmonica

accordion

VOICE

bass

ELECTRONIC INSTRUMENTS

synthesizer

PERCUSSION

drums

maraccas

Musical styles

blues	classical	country	folk	funk	hip hop
jazz	Latin	pop	rock	techno	worldbeat

3. Which selection did you prefer?

4. What type of music do you like to listen to?

5. What is your favourite instrument?

What did the guitar say to the guitarist?

Pick on someone your own size!

Did They Really Wear This?

In the 19th century, people dance

to live music only. They waltz in duets or in groups. Dancers wear top hats, evening gloves, and dresses with crinolines and jewellery.

In the 1920s, people love to have

fun and the most memorable dance of that decade is the Charleston. Women wear special dresses for dancing and men wear complete tuxedoes.

In the 1940s and 50s,

people still dress very well when they dance in ballrooms to the swinging sounds of the big bands. Men wear hats, tailored suits and shiny shoes. Women wear long ballroom gowns and their best jewels.

In the late 1950s, the rock and

roll generation begins to stand out from their parents' generation. Dance parties and popular music are now part of young people's lives. Some boys wear leather jackets, jeans and T-shirts. Girls wear long dresses or skirts with shirts and saddle shoes.

STEP 1

Do you think fashion is related to popular music? Is it important for a pop star to have his or her own style? Does their style influence you?

Before reading

1. **Look at** the pictures.

2. What do you think of the characters' clothes? Are they nice? Are they ugly?

Reading

3. **Read** the texts related to different **decades**.

decade: a 10-year period, the 1960s, the 1970s, etc.

glittering: sparkling, shiny.

top hat:

to waltz: to dance (a waltz).

In the 1960s' there is a lot of fashion action!
The British invasion brings in longer hair for men, lively colours, mini-skirts and wild patterns. Others choose to become hippies and protest against war wearing ponchos, bell-bottom pants, long hair, beards and sometimes... nothing at all!

The late 1970s and early 80s bring

glam rock, punk rock and disco. Hard rockers wear black T-shirts with black jeans. Some put on lots of make-up. Punks cut their hair Mohawk style. Disco dancers wear platform shoes, huge bell-bottom pants and glittering suits.

Finally, the 1980s brings
us the techno style of new wave music and the fashion that comes with it: short hair with highlights for men and women, some tight clothes and a weird mix of colours.

■ ■■■■ ■ ■■■■■

● ● ● ● ● ● ● ● ● ● ● ●

Reading *(continued)*

4. On your handout, **note** what people wear in each period.

5. What keyword helped you find what people wear in the text?

6. What is different or the same from one period to another?

After reading

7. What is your favourite fashion?

8. Do you think you would have followed any of these fashions?

Some people at my school ...

listen to... .

wear... .

TALK
ABOUT IT!

STRATEGY

See **Take notes**, p.193.

See **Compare**, p.188.

▼ Reinvest

9. Do you follow fashion and popular music styles?

10. Do any of your classmates wear old-fashioned clothes?

11. Describe what music is popular in your school.

12. Describe what some of your schoolmates are wearing. See Talk About It.

Eccentric But Brilliant

STEP 2

What makes an artist stand out from his peers? Is it something to do with talent and originality?

Before Reading

1. **Look at** the pictures.

2. What musical styles do these people play?

3. What type of texts are these?
   - biographies;
   - short stories;
   - letters.

Reading

4. **Read** the texts and **fill in** the chart on the handout.

BERRY, CHUCK (1926–)
Mr. Electric Guitar

Chuck Berry, *the father of rock and roll,* had a wild life. He had trouble with the law on the one hand and big success on the other. He was one of the first to play the electric guitar in a modern way. His famous song, *Johnny B. Goode,* was one of the tunes sent into space with the Voyager I spacecraft.

GOULD, GLENN (1932–1982)
A Great Pianist

Glenn Gould was a great Canadian pianist known all around the world. At the age of 32, in 1964, he stopped playing concerts, preferring to work only in the studio. He was one of the greatest interpreters of J. S. Bach. Gould was a strange person: he played piano sitting on a weird little chair that his father had made when he was young, and he often murmured both in concert and on recordings.

STRATEGY

See **Infer with cognates,** p.190.

Using adjectives to describe

When we describe people and things, we often use adjectives.

Ex. ... a **great classical** pianist...
He was **rich** and **famous**...

TALK ABOUT IT!

PRESLEY, ELVIS (1935–1977)
The "King"

Elvis was the one who really made rock & roll popular in America and around the world. He was so famous that, during all his career, he could not go out and live a normal life without attracting big crowds. A lot of his fans didn't believe in his death in 1977. They think he still lives and that he retired far from celebrity and show business.

After Reading

5. Which one of these artists do you think has had the most influence on music today?

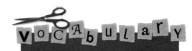

frivolous: not serious, silly.

gifted: having a special talent.

to murmur: to speak or sing softly.

to tour: to travel.

MOZART, WOLFGANG AMADEUS (1756–1791)
The Gifted Composer

Mozart wrote his first sonata at the age of 4. He spoke 15 languages by the time he was 6. He toured through all the European courts with his father and sister. He composed operas, symphonies, concertos and other works for a total of more than 600 compositions. He was rich and famous but also frivolous. He died at the age of 35, in debt, and was buried in a common grave.

▼ Reinvest

6. Do you know a special artist, musician or singer?

7. Briefly describe this special person to a classmate. See Talk About It.

1880 | 1910 | 1920

GRAMOPHONE

STEP 3 📄

Do you think that music is related to technology?

Before reading

1. **Look at** the texts on pages 68, 69 and 70.

2. **Scan** the texts to find dates and technological inventions.

Reading

3. **Read** the text and look for key sentences.

4. On you handout **write down** the important dates and inventions.

Music & Technology 📣))

1890–1930 The Recording Revolution

Human beings have built and played musical instruments since the dawn of time, using technology to do so. But in 1877, technology made history in the field of music. Thomas Edison made the first sound recording on a **phonograph**. The song was *Mary Had a Little Lamb*.

In 1885, the **gramophone** was introduced to the world. However, people had to wait a little while before having one in their homes.

In 1907, the **Victrola**, the first record player, went on sale to the public. This allowed people to listen to recordings made on 78-rpm vinyl records.

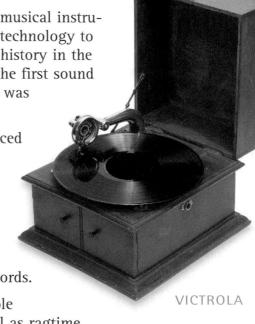

VICTROLA

Slowly, between 1914 and 1929, people discovered new popular songs, as well as ragtime, jazz and blues, not only in America, but also Europe and Asia.

STRATEGY

See **Scan**, p.192.

Telephone song

Play these tunes with a touch-tone phone. A comma (,) means a pause.

3212333, 222, 399, 3212333322321
Mary Had a Little Lamb

112163, 112196, 1108521, 008121
Happy Birthday

GIBSON ELECTRIC
GUITAR

VINYL
RECORD

1930–1960 The Radio Revolution

In 1931, Adolph Rickenbacker from Los Angeles,
California, built an **electric guitar.** In 1952, Gibson
produced its first solid-body (no empty space inside)
electric guitar.

In 1935, the first music and news **radio
station** started **broadcasting** in New York City.
By then, most families in America had
a radio receiver at home.

45-rpm **vinyl records** were used in multi-
record juke boxes. In 1950, young people
were listening to popular music like never before.

RADIO RECEIVER

Tape recording, used by the military,
became available to the music industry around 1948. After World War II,
hi-fi technology made **stereo sound**
possible.

STEREO PLAYER

VOCABULARY

century: 100 years.

broadcasting: sending
information using
a public media.

dawn of time: beginning
of everything.

hi-fi: high fidelity, clear
sound.

rpm: abbreviation for
rotations per minute.

significant: important.

to sing in key: to sing on
the exact notes.

CULTURE

If you want to **sing in
key,** pick up the
phone. Usually, the
tone you'll hear is a
medium "A" or "la".

Walkman and *Discman* are trademarks, names that are
used by people to designate music listening devices. Other
brand names like *Frigidaire, Kleenex, Gortex* and *Q-tips* are
also trademarked names. Their inventors gave them those
names.

AUDIO
COMPACT
DISC

MP3 PLAYER

After reading

5. In your opinion, what was the most **significant** technology used in the music industry in the last **century**?

6. What period do you think was the most important?

7. Name a technology we still use today.

1960–2000 The Digital Revolution

In 1966, Robert Moog started selling his huge **synthesizers**. Four years later, he made a portable version of this unique musical instrument.

In 1979, Sony introduced the very first **portable audio cassette player** or "Walkman." People could listen to music anywhere. In 1982, Sony and Philips introduced the **audio compact disc** and the "Discman." It was the beginning of the digital era in music.

In 1997, Michael Robertson and his team developed the **MP3 format**. This very small computer file format made it possible to digitize songs and share them on computers.

Artists are facing a huge problem; most people can listen to their music without buying it or paying for it.

Technology is still changing music. Or is it the other way around? Only time will tell.

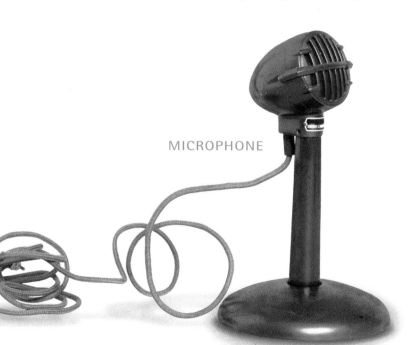

MICROPHONE

▼ Reinvest

8. In teams, **draw** a timeline showing the evolution of music and technology between 1890 and 2000. ✏️➡

9. Present your timeline to your classmates.

10. Tell them which invention was the most significant in your opinion.

Song or Poem? 🔊

English Project Blues

Verse 1
Tomorrow's the presentation,
We have no idea what to do.
The teacher wants a good interpretation,
Or else we won't get our due.

chorus
My project, my teamwork, it all went wrong!

Verse 2
Brainstorming with my teammates,
Our thoughts in nothing culminate.
I hope we'll be up to it,
Because I'll never see the end of it.

chorus
My project, my teamwork, it all went wrong!

Verse 3
My teacher tells me I have to learn,
Working in a team, teaches respect.
We all want the attention we earn,
This is after all what we expect.

chorus
My project, my teamwork, it all went wrong!

Verse 4
I just came back from school,
It's all right, I have good news.
My team and I are glad,
It won't be a fad.

chorus
My project, my teamwork, it all went all right!
My project, my teamwork, it all went all right!

"Big Blues Ben" JARET

STEP 4

What is the difference between the **lyrics** of a song and a poem? Do lyrics usually use rhyme?

Before reading

1. **Scan** the text to look at its structure.

2. How many sections are there in the song?

Reading

3. **Read** the lyrics.

4. What is the song about?
   • homeworks;
   • love;
   • school life.

5. What are the two main sections of a song?

After reading

6. Do you understand the lyrics?

7. Are lyrics important in a song?

VOCABULARY

| **due:** something that is merited. | **to earn:** to get something one merits. | **fad:** something very popular for a very short time. | **lyrics:** words in a song. |

▼ Reinvest

8. What do songs talk about today? Do they talk about love, society, personal problems, solutions, and the environment?

9. Write down the title of your Top-3 favourite songs. ◀▬▬✏▶

10. Present your favourite song to your classmates.

STRATEGY

See **Infer with contextual cues**, p.191.

Centuries, Decades and Music

1720–1840
The Baroque and Classical Periods

1725
Vivaldi writes *The Four Seasons.*

1742
Handel's *Messiah* is first played.

1750
J. S. Bach dies, the Baroque period ends.

1786
Mozart's *The Marriage of Figaro* premieres in Vienna.

1807
Beethoven writes his *Symphony #5.*

1825–1918
The Romantic and Impressionist Periods

1843
Richard Wagner presents his opera *The Ghost Ship.*

1850
The golden age of piano.

1867
Johann Strauss writes his famous waltz *The Blue Danube.*

1877
Thomas Edison invents the phonograph.

1905
Debussy composes *La mer.*

1890–1960
The Blues, Jazz and Swing Periods

1890
Former Afro-American slaves introduce the blues.

1913
Billboard publishes the most famous vaudeville songs.

1919
Chicago becomes the Jazz City.

1932
Duke Ellington marks the debut of swing.

1936
The electric guitar is born.

vocabulary

craze: something very popular for a short time.

era: a period of history or time.

to premiere: to present something for the first time (a film, a play).

slave: a person owned by another person.

▼ Reinvest

An Artist's Timeline   **PROJECT A**

In this project, you will choose a specific artist from any time and place and create a timeline with the information you find in magazines, encyclopedias, websites, etc. You should also include events in the timeline that help us understand the period.

Red	Orange	Green
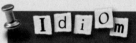 Technological event.	Important song, album or dance.	Interesting event or fact.

1950–1970
The Rock and Roll Era

1948

The 33 ⅓-rpm LP is created with 25 minutes of music per side.

1951

Rhythm and blues is transformed into rock and roll.

1956

Elvis Presley becomes the first rock and roll star.

1963

Beatlemania takes Britain by storm. The Rolling Stones quickly follow.

1969

The Woodstock rock festival is held in New York state.

1971–1999
An Explosion of Styles and the Video Era

1974

Hey Joe, the first punk rock song is released.

1956

The blockbuster movie *Saturday Night Fever* opens the disco era.

1983

The compact disk is introduced.

1996

La Macarena is the biggest dance craze since *The Twist*.

1999

By the end of the century, five big corporations control the music business.

Reading *(continued)*

5. Where can you find out what the coloured fonts mean?

6. How many different **eras** does the time-line show?

After reading

7. In your opinion, which of these events is the most important in musical history?

8. Which event seems the least important?

Idiom

a golden age:

a very important period

A Musical Survey   PROJECT B

To create a good survey, you need questions about music. In your project, don't forget to include questions about habits, musical styles and genres, as well as preferences and a chart to sum up your information.

The Radio Host 🔊

Project C
Getting Started

Do you listen to the radio? If so, when do you listen to the radio?

Before Reading

1. **Look at** the comic strip.

2. **What is** the character in the comic strip doing?

3. **What is** his job?

Reading

4. **Read** the comic strip.

5. **Match** each square with the appropriate subtitle.

The news.

Getting the show started.

The weather.

The interview (over the phone).

Sports.

Music.

Traffic report.

Arts and Goodbyes.

A Welcome to your favourite morning show. I'm your host: Mike Rofone.

B Wow. What a nice day!

Outside: -24 °C

Inside: 22 °C

C Welcome to our show, Mrs. Prime Minister.

D A car accident... A peace treaty...

Radio News

E
Listen up! This is the latest #1 hit on the charts.

F
Code red almost everywhere this morning.

G
And now, yesterday's game scores.

H
That's it for us folks!

After reading

6. There is a lot to talk about in a radio show.

   In your opinion, what are the most important subjects?

7. Do you listen to this type of radio show?

▼ **Reinvest**

PROJECT C

A Radio Show

In this project, you will create your own radio capsule. You will first need to decide what you are going to talk about. Listen to the radio and select some useful lines to help you out.

Promotion Is the Key

Project D
Getting Started

What is the best way to promote something like a concert?

Before Reading

1. **Skim** through all the promotional tools.

2. At first sight, which promotional tool do you like best?

Reading

3. **Read** through each promotional tool and **examine it closely.**

4. What event is being promoted?

5. **Match** each tool with the appropriate name. See **Word Bank**.

After reading

6. **Imagine** you have to promote a show in your school. Which of these promotional tools would you choose?

7. What makes good promotional material?

Tool #1

prices: $49 to $79. Civic Arena, March 15th at 7 p.m. doors open at 6 p.m.

Tool #2

Don't forget to listen to our special show.

Resl RADIO

I know I will!

Tool #3

CIVIC ARENA

no

IN CONCERT

MARCH 15th at 7 P.M.
Prices: $49 to $79
Doors open at 6 P.M.

Tool #4

Would you like to hear our new album?

Wow it's really great. When are you doing your next show?

Tomorrow night. Would you like to buy a ticket?

Sure. I'll take two tickets and a CD.

word bank

| flyer | poster | stand | sandwich man |

▼ **Reinvest**

Promote Your Own Show

PROJECT D

What would you like to promote? A radio show? A concert? A band?

In this project, you will produce a promotional tool that fits your needs and will work for your audience.

Your Project Presentation

- Did you work individually or in teams?

- Was each task you had to do clear?

- How much time did you spend on your project?

- Did your project require more work than you expected?

- Do you need more time to rehearse in order to prepare for your presentation?

- Do you have all the material you need for the presentation?

- Which part of the project do you find the most interesting: the preparation, the carrying-out of the project or its presentation?

It's time to present your project.

Speak clearly, use gestures and stall for time when you hesitate on a word or expression.

Your Portfolio

During this unit, you experienced a lot of different activities related to music, the history of music, musicians and technology, etc. You learned to use some new words and expressions; you learned to use new strategies when inter-acting orally, reading or listening to texts.

Be sure to put the following items in your portfolio:

- The *In this Unit* handout, to self-evaluate your learning in relation to oral interactions, texts and stategies.

- All the notes and short texts you wrote in the Reinvest section at the end of some of the activities.

- The *Vocabulary* and *Language* handouts that you completed.

- The *Evaluation* handouts you completed.

- Any texts, documents or pictures that can help you present your project.

Bits and Bites

Find the secret letters in the picture.

Using these letters, **spell** as many names of fruits and vegetables as you know.

■ Note: You may use each letter more than once.

IN THIS UNIT
You Will...

- discuss your eating habits;
- discover a farmer's market;
- learn an easy recipe;
- find out about the origin of some foods;
- plan a budget;
- practice ordering food.

Text Types
Look at, read and/or listen to...
questionnaires, recipes, menus, supermarket flyers, information-based articles, biographies and a comic strip.

Strategies
- predict with pictures;
- pay selective attention;
- practise;
- scan;
- infer with cognates.

Projects
Write or produce one of the following projects:
- *History and Food;*
- *At the Restaurant;*
- *Great Menus.*

Activity 1

Do you eat well?
What are your eating
habits?

1. Read the questions
on this page.

2. Write down
your answers in your
notebook.

canned:

takeout:

twice: two times.

whole-wheat:

What Do You Eat?

QUESTIONS

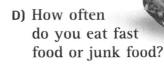

A) Which vegetables do you eat
the most often?

❶ canned vegetables.

❷ frozen vegetables.

❸ fresh vegetables.

B) What type
of bread do
you eat on a
regular basis?

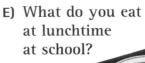

❶ white bread.

❷ freshly baked baguette.

❸ whole-wheat bread.

C) What type of pizza do you eat
the most often?

❶ frozen pizza.

❷ takeout pizza.

❸ homemade pizza.

D) How often
do you eat fast
food or junk food?

❶ twice a week or more.

❷ once a week.

❸ once a month.

E) What do you eat
at lunchtime
at school?

❶ I don't eat lunch.

❷ cafeteria or fast food.

❸ a homemade lunch.

F) How often do you eat
candies?

❶ every day.

❷ 2 or 3 times a week.

❸ once a week.

SCORES

If your score is between 25 and 30

Bravo! You go for fresh and natural food! That is wonderful! You know what to eat and you have good eating habits. We are what we eat. You're a smart eater!

If your score is between 18 and 24

Not so good. You can improve your eating habits. Eat more fresh vegetables and fruits. Avoid fatty, salty or sugary food. You will have more energy and more concentration at school. A good diet is a bonus!

If your score is between 6 and 17

You're in serious trouble, my friend! Change your eating habits right away! You need good food for your bones, muscles and brain. What type of body do you want? Think about it!

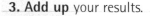

3. **Add up** your results.
   Answers ❶ = 1 point;
   Answers ❷ = 3 points;
   Answers ❸ = 5 points.

4. **Find out** what your score tells you about your eating habits.

5. Do you have good eating habits?
   See **Talk About It.**

CULTURE

"Junk food"

Fast food became popular in North America during the 1950s. Since then, fast-food restaurants have spread all over the world.

People like fast food because it is quick, tasty and inexpensive. However, it contains fat, salt, sugar and chemical substances. This is bad for human health. That's why it is often called *"junk food."*

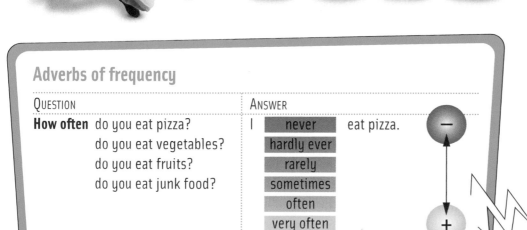

Adverbs of frequency

QUESTION	ANSWER
How often do you eat pizza?	I never eat pizza.
do you eat vegetables?	hardly ever
do you eat fruits?	rarely
do you eat junk food?	sometimes
	often
	very often

TALK ABOUT IT!

I Went to the Market

Activity 2

Have you ever been to a farmer's market? What can you find there?

1. Look at the pictures.

2. Make a list of the food products you can see...

- ...at the fruit and vegetable stand;
- ...at the cheese shop;
- ...at the fish market;
- ...at the meat market;
- ...at the bakery shop.

> ROGERS' FARM

> THE CHEESY-WAY

> I would like two heads of lettuce.

> Do you have feta cheese?

> Are your mussels fresh?

> How much are these red onions?

> I need a **pound** of Parmesan cheese, please.

> Give me a basket of those apples, please.

> I want 500 grams of coffee. Very fine, please.

> What's on sale today?

What is worse than finding a worm in your food?

Finding only half a worm.

3. **Compare** your list with a classmate's.

4. **Ask** what your class-mate found in each stand or shop.
See **Talk About It.**

CULTURE

1 Kg = 2.2 pounds

A **pound** equals 454 grams. The symbol for a **pound** is **lb.** The pound is the unit of weight in the imperial system and it is still used in the United States.

The kilogram is a unit of mass. It replaced the **pound** in the 1970s in Canada. It is part of the international system of measures used in most countries around the world.

This grain fed chicken please, and ten of those merguez sausages.

I'm number 23. I want a sourdough sunflower baguette and four Kaiser rolls.

How much is your chocolate mousse cake?

QUESTION	ANSWER
What did you find at ... the bakery shop?	At the bakery shop, I found bread and pastries.
... the fruit and vegetable stand?	
... etc.	

TALK ABOUT IT!

Banana and Chocolate Muffins

STEP 1

Do you like muffins? Would you like to try this recipe?

Before reading

1. **Name** the two sections of the recipe.

2. In which section will you find the cooking instructions?

3. In which section will you find the quantities you need for cooking?

Reading

4. **Read** the recipe.

5. **Put** the directions in the correct order using the letters.

Listening

6. **Listen** to the recipe and verify your answers.

After listening

7. Are your directions in the correct order?

Ingredients

- 85 ml ($\frac{1}{3}$ cup) of vegetable oil
- 125 ml ($\frac{1}{2}$ cup) of brown sugar
- 1 egg, beaten
- 2 ripe bananas, mashed
- 250 ml (1 cup) of semi-sweet chocolate chips

- 250 ml (1 cup) of flour
- 125 ml ($\frac{1}{2}$ cup) of oatmeal
- 5 ml (1 tsp.) of baking soda
- 3 ml (a pinch) of salt
- 3 ml (a pinch) of cinnamon

Discourse markers

The words **first, then, after, at the same time, now, next, later** and **finally** are very useful for marking the sequence of an event or a task.

Example: **The 4 p.m. Tea Break**

First, you boil the water.
Next, put a teabag in a teapot.
After that, pour some boiling water in the teapot.
Then, let the tea steep for a few minutes.
Finally, pour the tea in a teacup and enjoy!

TALK ABOUT IT!

Directions

A) **Put** the mixture in a greased muffin pan and **bake** at 200°C (400°F), for 15 to 20 minutes.

B) In another bowl, **mix** the dry ingredients: the flour, oatmeal, baking soda, salt and cinnamon.

C) **Beat** the oil, sugar and egg together in a bowl.

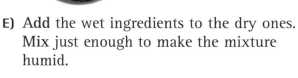

D) **Add** the bananas and chocolate chips.

E) **Add** the wet ingredients to the dry ones. Mix just enough to make the mixture humid.

STRATEGY

See **Predict** with pictures, p. 187.

▼ Reinvest

8. **Give** the directions for the recipe to a classmate in the correct order.

9. **Use** *discourse markers* to be more precise. See Talk About It.

10. **Give** the directions for a recipe you know to a classmate.

beaten:

mashed:

pinch: a small amount.

ripe: ready to be eaten.

tsp. (abbreviation of teaspoon):

Tongue twisters

Repeat these sentences ten times, really fast:

- Betty baked a better batch of buttered cookies.

- Chef chopped cheese chunks cheerfully.

Rosie's Cafe

STEP 2

Do you often order from a takeout? What do you like to order? Do you usually order healthy food?

Before listening

1. **Look at** the menu from *Rosie's Cafe.*

Listening

2. **Listen to** what William and Fanny order.

3. **Fill out** the order on the handout.

STRATEGY

See **Pay selective attention**, p. 184.
See **Practise**, p.189.

Rosie's Cafe

5467 1st Avenue, Cape Jay
FREE DELIVERY: every day from 11 a.m. to 4 p.m.
Phone: (412) 894-9911

Pastas

Spaghetti carbonara	$8.95
Fettucine Alfredo	$9.95
Tortellini rosé	$8.95

Pitas*

Souvlaki (pork)	$4.25
Chicken	$4.75
Vegetarian	$4.25

Sandwiches*
(white or brown bread)

BLT	$4.50
(bacon, lettuce and tomato)	
Salmon or tuna	$4.75
Club	$7.95

From the Grill

Plate of baby back ribs	$10.95
1/2 portion of baby back ribs	$8.95
Chicken leg with baby back ribs	$10.25
Marinated chicken breast	$8.25
Chicken brochette	$8.25

Salads

	small	large
Chef's salad	$5.95	$6.95
Greek salad	$6.95	$8.50
Caesar salad	$8.50	$10.95

Extras

Coleslaw	$1.75
Soup	$1.95
Vegetable plate	$1.50

Beverages

Soft drinks	$1.25
Orange, apple or tomato juice	$1.50
Milk shakes	$4.25
Tea, coffee	$1.50

Desserts

Ice cream	$2.25
Rice pudding	$2.50
Chocolate cake	$3.25

*Pitas and sandwiches are served with chef's salad.

WAITER OR WAITRESS	CUSTOMER

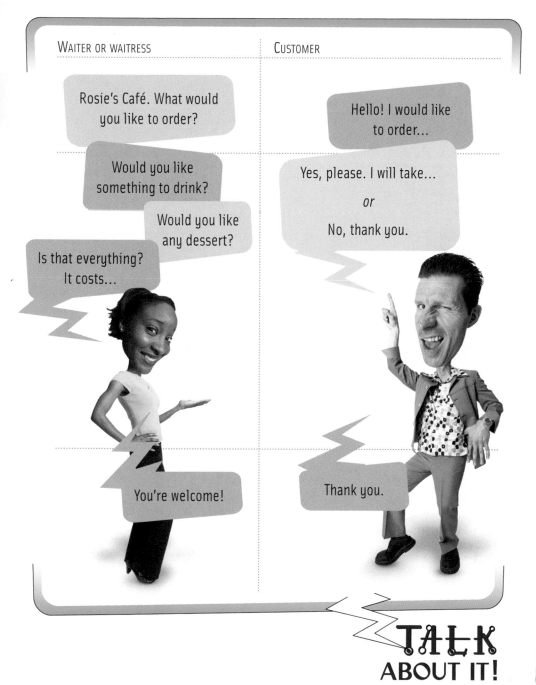

WAITER OR WAITRESS

Rosie's Café. What would you like to order?

Would you like something to drink?

Would you like any dessert?

Is that everything? It costs...

You're welcome!

CUSTOMER

Hello! I would like to order...

Yes, please. I will take...

or

No, thank you.

Thank you.

TALK ABOUT IT!

CULTURE

The origin of hotdogs

A dachshund is a breed of dog and also a type of sausage. Dachshund sandwiches were popular in America. They were eaten at baseball games.

In 1901, a famous cartoonist named Mr. Dorgan, drew barking dogs in bread rolls. And because he could not spell "dachshund," he called them "**hot dogs**."

▼ **Reinvest**

6. a) **Team up** with a classmate.

   b) **Decide** who will order (the customer) and who will take the order (waiter or waitress). See **Talk About It.**

   c) **Interact** orally as if you were on the phone.

Budgeting

Do you shop for food with your parents? Do you know what the healthier choices are?

Before Reading

1. **Look at** the flyers.

2. Do you recognize these items?

3. Which items do you like or dislike?

Reading

4. **Read** the flyers.

5. **Draw** a table in your notebook. ✏➤

Breakfast	Lunch	Snack	Dinner

6. **Write down** the name of each item in the correct column. ✏➤

A
$1⁹⁹

B
$3⁹⁹

C
$2⁹⁹

D Cinnamon-sugared buns

6 for $2⁹⁹

E Oatmeal and date muffins

6 for $2⁹⁹

F Whole-wheat, multi-grain, bran, white
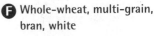
$2⁴⁹

G
$1⁹⁹

H
$4⁹⁹

I
$4⁹⁹

J
$2⁹⁹

K
$2³⁹

L Half, boneless, smoked ham, ready to eat (approx. 2.5 kg)

$2⁵⁴ kg

M Ground beef

$6⁵⁹ kg

N Fresh Atlantic salmon steaks

$9⁹⁰ kg

O Black Forest ham

$9⁹⁰ kg

P Chicken legs

$3⁵¹ kg

Q Red organic tomatoes

5 for $2¹⁸

R Quebec-grown, washed, white potatoes

$0.⁹⁹ 5 kg

S Granny Smith apples

6 for $1⁹⁶

T

CORN
14 oz 398 ml
GREEN BEANS 14 oz 398 ml
GREEN PEAS 14 oz 398 ml
YELLOW

3 for $1⁹⁹

●●●●●●●●●●●●●●

After Reading

7. For which items do you have to estimate the price?

CULTURE

Organic food is food that is grown naturally, without any chemical fertilizers, antibiotics or pesticides.

▼ **Reinvest**

8. What would you buy if you needed to feed four people for a day, with a budget of 25 dollars?

9. Choose food for each meal. Try to make healthy choices.

10. Present your meals to classmates.

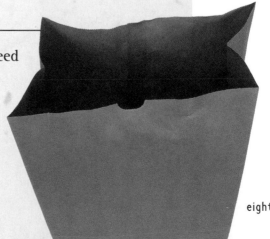

Food and Celebration

STEP 4

Celebration and food go together. Celebrations often have religious meanings.

Before Reading

1. **Look at** the subtitles in the text.

2. What do they represent?
   - birthdays;
   - celebrations;
   - festivals;
   - holidays.

American Thanksgiving

This traditional American celebration has its origin the beginning of the 13 British Colonies of North America. The Pilgrim Fathers, who were English immigrants, travelled in 1620 on a ship called the *Mayflower*. After a difficult year in the colonies, the Pilgrims had their first harvest and organised a feast. Together with local Amerindians, they ate goose, turkey, squash, corn and beans. At the same time, they expressed the fact that they were grateful for all this food. That is why Americans still celebrate Thanksgiving with a turkey dinner.

Mardi Gras

Mardi Gras is an old Christian celebration. It precedes a 40-day long fast before Easter. At Mardi Gras, people eat generous helpings of food like cream, butter, sugar and pastries. In New Orleans, Louisiana, people still celebrate Mardi Gras with a huge parade. They eat a dessert called "King Cake." It tastes like a coffee cake. It is decorated in purple, green and gold. Inside, there is a special baby doll. If you get it, you will have to organise the next Mardi Gras party.

STRATEGY

See **Scan**, p. 192.
See **Infer with cognates**, p.190.

I **would like to** try some baklava.

I **would like to** try the King cake.

TALK ABOUT IT!

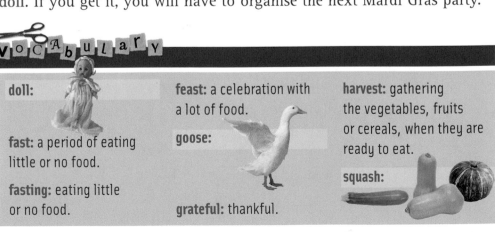

Vocabulary

doll:

fast: a period of eating little or no food.

fasting: eating little or no food.

feast: a celebration with a lot of food.

goose:

grateful: thankful.

harvest: gathering the vegetables, fruits or cereals, when they are ready to eat.

squash:

Passover

Passover, or *Pesach*, celebrates the historic Jewish escape from Egypt about 3,200 years ago. The Jewish people were slaves under the pharaoh in those ancient times. The *Seder* is the ritual Passover dinner, symbolic of their escape.

Jewish people eat food cooked in salted water. This is symbolic of their tears. They eat green spring vegetables, like asparagus, peas, parsley. They eat a bread called *matzoth*, the "bread of freedom." It is a big, square, flat cracker. The bread is hard because it symbolizes that being free is not easy.

Ramadan

Ramadan is the holiest month in the Islamic calendar. During Ramadan, Muslims fast and pray during daylight hours. They do not eat from sun-up to sun-down. Both rich and poor observe Ramadan. In this way, everyone knows how it feels to be hungry. After a month of fasting, Muslims have a wonderful feast. They sing, dance and play games. They eat sweet food: dates, candies, cookies and pastries such as baklava.

▼ Reinvest

8. Ask your classmates about the food they eat during their celebrations.

9. Which food would you like to try? See **Talk About It.**

Reading

3. **Read** all four texts.

4. **Scan** each text to find out what food is associated with each celebration.

After Reading

5. Do you participate in one of these celebrations? Do you know any other celebrations?

6. **Name** some of your family or cultural celebrations.

7. **Name** any special foods or meals you eat during these celebrations.

Why did they let the turkey join the band?

Because he had the drum-sticks.

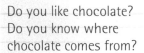

STEP 5 📄

Do you like chocolate?
Do you know where
chocolate comes from?

Before reading

1. **Read** the three
   different text titles.

2. Which title do
   you think indicates
   a biography?

Reading

3. **Read** all three texts.

4. On the handout, **write
   down** all the impor-
   tant information on
   the timeline.

The History of Chocolate

The Drink of the Gods

Chocolate is made with cocoa beans. The Aztecs, Incas and Mayas all used to make a drink with chocolate. It was called "the drink of the gods." They mixed cocoa beans with spices, corn and even bees. They believed it could **cure** illness.

Chocolate Travels to Europe

In the 16th century, Spanish conquistadors brought chocolate to Europe. In the 18th century, hot chocolate became a fashionable drink among Spanish and other European aristocrats. It was considered a luxurious treat.

In the 19th Century

In England, the Cadbury family created industrial chocolate. They promoted the idea of drinking chocolate instead of alcoholic beverages. In the United States, James Baker founded his company and Milton S. Hershey manufactured the first commercial chocolate bars.

Cocoa fruit

Real Chocolate

Candied or industrial chocolate is different from handmade chocolate. Chocolate bars have lots of other ingredients in them and taste more like sugar than cocoa. But it is possible to taste real chocolate around the world. Chocolate makers continue the tradition of producing fine chocolates. Chocolate lovers have founded clubs and societies to celebrate this gift from nature.

vocabulary

apothecary: pharmacist.

bitter: a sharp, sometimes unpleasant taste like coffee.

confectioner: a maker of candies.

to cure: to help a sick person get better.

The Story of Suchard

Chocolate for his Mother

There was once a little boy named Philippe Suchard. He lived in Switzerland. In 1809, when he was still young, his mother became ill. The doctor said that the best way to cure his mother's illness was to eat chocolate. So, Philippe's father sent him to the apothecary to buy a pound of chocolate. Chocolate was very expensive. An average workman would work three days to pay for a pound of chocolate.

Becoming a Confectioner

One day, Philippe left home to go to work. His brother was a **confectioner** and Philippe learned his craft. In 1825, he opened his own shop and invented a chocolate lozenge, the *diablotin*. This chocolate became a favourite among the people of Neuchâtel, Switzerland.

Becoming a Famous Chocolate Maker

In 1851, Philippe decided to present his chocolates at the Great Exhibition in London. It was a real success. He succeeded again four years later in Paris, in 1855. His chocolates won all the gold medals, making his *diablotin* famous around the world.

Mayan Chocolate

In 1554, a delegation of Mayas from Guatemala brought a few surprises to the Spanish court. The Mayas gave the Prince many gifts. They offered rare feathers, corn and chocolate. But the story doesn't say if the royal family enjoyed the chocolate. After all, the "royal drink" was not such a delicious beverage at first because of its bitterness.

Reading (continued)

5. Which two texts have the same information about the Mayas and chocolate?

After reading

6. Which of the three texts do you prefer?

7. **Name** three things you learned about chocolate.

CULTURE

Some historians believe that the word chocolate comes from the Aztec word *xocoalt, xoco* meaning **bitter** and *alt* meaning water. This makes sense because chocolate was used to make a drink.

▼ **Reinvest**

You now know that cocoa is in fact **bitter**, not sweet. Other foods may also have different tastes: sweet, salty or sour.

8. **Name** ten beverages you know.

9. **Say** what they taste like.

History of Food

Project A 📝
Getting Started

Our food comes from all over the world. Do you know the origins of some of your favourite foods?

Before Reading

1. **Fill in** the handout and guess where each food comes from.

2. **Look at** the map and pictures.

3. Which of these foods are **neither** a fruit **nor** a vegetable?

Reading

4. **Read** the texts on the map.

5. The origin of the oranges and the onions are uncertain. Which word tells you that?

Cranberries are native to eastern North America. The Algonquins called them atoqua (good fruit). British Columbia is Canada's largest producer of cranberries.

Vanilla comes from a flower which grows in Mexico. The Aztecs used vanilla to flavour their chocolate drinks. The conquistador Cortez brought it to Europe in the 16th century. Vanilla is the most popular flavouring in the world.

NORTH AMERICA

ATLANTIC OCEAN

CENTRAL AMERICA

Corn was called *maize* by Amerindians, who used to grow it all over the Americas. Christopher Columbus first saw corn in Cuba and brought it back to Europe.

PACIFIC OCEAN

SOUTH AMERICA

The **potato** is native to the Andes Mountains in Peru and Bolivia. It was cultivated there 2,400 years ago. It arrived in Europe around 1534, but was not really cooked until a French chef named Parmentier introduced it to King Louis XVI around 1780.

What did the computer do at lunchtime?

It had a byte to eat!

Kiwis are native to Siberia, China, Korea and Japan. There are 55 different species of kiwis. They are rich in vitamins A and C, as well as fibre and calcium.

ASIA

EUROPE

Pasta was eaten by the **Etruscans** and the Romans in Antiquity. Marco Polo did not bring it back from China. This is a myth. Dried pasta became popular in the 14th and 15th centuries. It was easy to store on ships. Italian boats made long commercial trips to the Americas.

Oranges probably come from China. Italian merchants brought them back to Europe. Oranges are the most commonly grown fruit trees in the world.

AFRICA

INDIAN OCEAN

OCEANIA

Onions are one of the oldest of **crops**. They probably came from Egypt originally. The people who built the pyramids ate onions. They believed that onions gave them strength. Roman soldiers ate them before going into battle.

ANTARTIC OCEAN

ANTARTICA

After reading

6. **Check** the handout to see how many answers you knew or guessed correctly.

7. Which text surprised you the most?

Vocabulary

crop: vegetables, fruits, cereals or other plants grown in fields.

Etruscans: an ancient tribe who lived in Italy before the time of the Romans.

neither... nor: not the one or the other.

▼ **Reinvest**

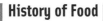

History of Food | **PROJECT A**

How about looking for the origins of a food you like? In your project, you will have to present:
- The country of origin of the food you choose;
- The date, period and people involved in the history of that food;
- The way the food is grown or prepared.

At the Restaurant

●●●●●●●●●●●●●●●

Project B
Getting Started

Do you like going to restaurants? What is your favourite restaurant?

Before Reading

1. **Look at** the pictures.

2. What type of restaurant is it?

   - a gourmet restaurant;

   - a junk-food restaurant;

   - a family restaurant.

Reading

3. **Team up** with two classmates.

4. **Read** the comic strip together, each playing one of the parts.

Good evening! How are you?

What would you recommend tonight?

Good evening! Fine, thank you.

Well... the seafood pasta is very good. The fresh Atlantic salmon is very fresh.

That sounds excellent!

Would you like something to drink while you decide?

May I have a glass of soda water?

May I have tomato juice, please?

Sorry we don't have any more tomato juice.

Yes sir, we do.

Do you have any orange juice.

Then, I'll have one please.

Are you ready to order?

Yes we are.

I would like the salmon, please. Does the special come with the soup?

Yes miss, the soup and the dessert are included.

I would like the soup too. I would like the pasta, because I like seafood. Could I have extra seafood?

Of course you can, no problem.

So, it's salmon for the lady and pasta with extra seafood for the gentleman.

That's correct. May we have another basket of bread?

I'll bring one back in a minute.

Waiter, waiter!!

What's the problem miss?

Th... th... there is a fly in my soup.

That's okay miss, there's no extra charge. It's included in the special. Bon appetit!

After Reading

5. Which character did you prefer?

6. How did you like the end of the story?
   • bizarre;
   • funny;
   • possible;
   • fictional.

7. Did something like that ever happen to you?

STRATEGY

See **Practise**, p. 189.

PROJECT B

At the Restaurant: A Skit

You can act out this comic strip in order to practise some dialogue.

Imagine a new skit in which you will include:

• Social conventions like salutations, leave-taking, permission and fillers;

• The kind of restaurant and menu you prefer;

• A surprising ending, if possible.

Menus For All

Project C
Getting Started

Are there many different kinds of restaurants in your region? Do you cook meals at home?

Before Reading

1. **Look at** these table d'hôte menus.

2. **Guess** what kind of restaurant they come from.

Reading

3. **Read** the names of the restaurants and the menus.

4. Which menu comes from...
   • a Chinese restaurant?
   • an Italian restaurant?
   • an Indian restaurant?

5. While reading, find the most and the least expensive menus.

After reading

6. Which menu do you prefer?

7. What would you order?

Restaurant Patha

Soups and appetizers: Dahl soup

Chef's special: Chicken tikka masala, Butter chicken or Shrimp balachaw

*Tandoori dishes: Tandoori chicken, Lamb tikka or Tandoori platter

Desserts: Melon and strawberry salad or Rice pudding

Tea

$19.95 per person

---

*Tandoori dishes are served with basmati rice or nan bread, green salad and mint sauce.

Restaurant Marco Pavoni

Soups and antipasti:
Chicken soup, minestrone or prosciutto and melon

Spaghetti marinara, fettuccine Alfredo or seafood risotto

Veal pizzaiola, lamb Bella Napoli or filet of sole in marsala sauce

Salads:
green salad or mixed tomato salad

Dessert: Tiramisu

Tea or coffee

$39.95 per person

EGG ROLL PALACE

FULL COURSE MEAL

• Egg rolls (3 per person)
• Pineapple chicken or beef macaroni
• Dry spareribs or sweet and sour shrimps

• Chicken chow mein
• Chicken fried rice
• Almond cookies

For 1: $11.50   For 2: $15.50

 **Great Menus**   **PROJECT C**

It's time to prepare your own favourite menu.
• You should include the soups and/or appetizers, the main courses, and finally, the desserts.
• Present your menu with a choice of fonts and presentation that suits your type of restaurant.
• Write a short description of each main course.

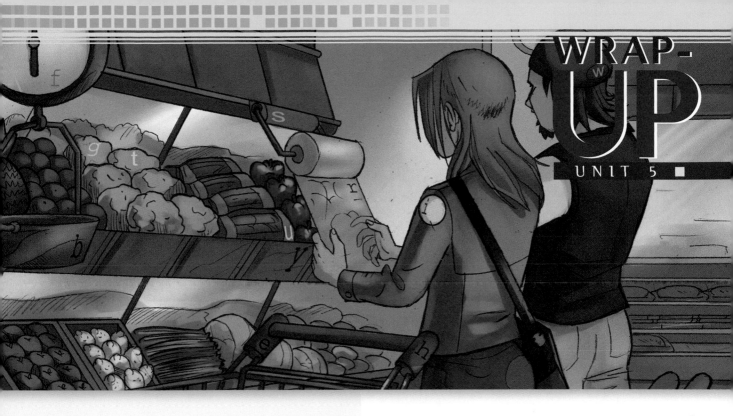

Your Project Presentation

- • Did you work individually or in a team?

- • Was it clear what you had to do for each task?

- • How much time did you spend on your project?

- • What was the easiest task you had to do for your project? The most difficult?

- • Do you have all the material you need for the presentation?

- • Which part of the project do you find the most interesting: the preparation, the carrying-out of the project or its presentation?

It's time to present your project.

Speak clearly, use gestures and stall for time if you find yourself hesitating on a word or expression.

Your Portfolio

During this unit, you experienced a lot of different activities related to food, the history of certain foods, and ordering in a restaurant or a take-out, etc. You learned to use some new words and expressions; you learned to use new strategies when interacting orally, or reading and listening to texts.

Be sure to put the following items in your portfolio:

- • The *In this Unit* handout, to self-evaluate your learning in relation to oral interactions and strategies.

- • All the notes and short texts you wrote in the Reinvest section at the end of some of the activities.

  - • The *Vocabulary* and *Language* handouts that you completed.

  - • The *Evaluation* handouts you completed.

  - • Any texts, documents or pictures that can help you present your project.

Are You Ready To Play?

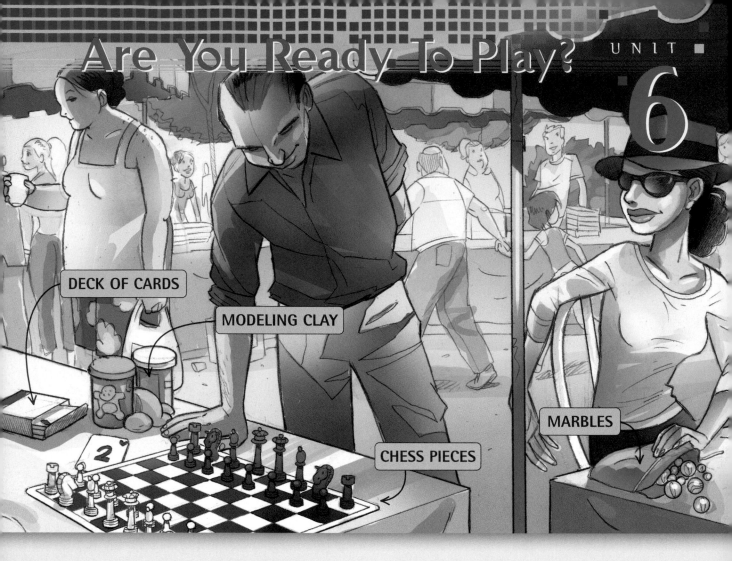

DECK OF CARDS

MODELING CLAY

MARBLES

CHESS PIECES

1. **Read** the riddles.

2. **Look at** the pictures and the clues to find the answers.

A
We always come in pairs.
Usually, we are black and white.
We are very old, about 1,000 years.
What are we?

B
We are a family of fifty-two plus two funny guys.
We only have two dimensions.
We are a royal family.
What are we?

C
We originally came from India.
We can go up or down.
We sometimes hiss.
What are we?

D
We are made from glass.
We have different colours.
Don't step on us or you'll fall.
What are we?

E
We are two royal families.
We all walk differently.
We like to "check" and "mate" each other.
What are we?

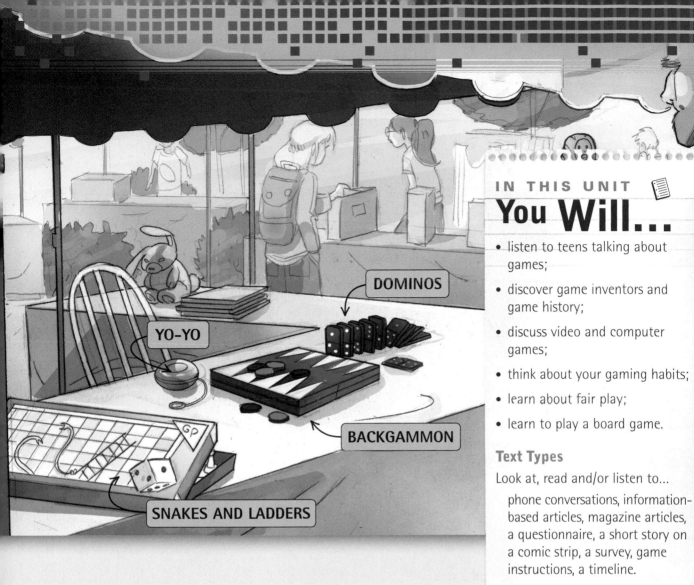

DOMINOS

YO-YO

BACKGAMMON

SNAKES AND LADDERS

IN THIS UNIT

You Will...

- listen to teens talking about games;

- discover game inventors and game history;

- discuss video and computer games;

- think about your gaming habits;

- learn about fair play;

- learn to play a board game.

Text Types

Look at, read and/or listen to...

phone conversations, information-based articles, magazine articles, a questionnaire, a short story on a comic strip, a survey, game instructions, a timeline.

Strategies

- pay selective attention;

- compare;

- predict;

- encourage self and others;

- skim.

Projects

Write or produce one of the following projects:

- *A Game Survey*;

- *History of a Game*;

- *A Game Tournament*.

F

I can be whatever you want.
I come in different colours.
Sometimes I smell like fruit.
What am I?

I can be made of wood, metal or plastic.
I have a string and I go up and down.
My name means "come, come".
What am I?

G

We come with 24 arrows and two dice.
We wear red and black.
Bring us home.
What are we?

H

A Rainy Day

Activity 1

A nice weekend can be ruined when rain comes down. Good thing we have indoor games that we can play.

1. **Listen to** the conversation between Jane and Helen.

2. **Pay attention** to the greetings and farewells they use.

3. **Note down** the names of the games they talk about. ✏️

4. What do you do when it is raining outside? See **Write About it** on the next page.

Greetings

Hi.

Hey.

How are you?

Hello.

Good morning. / Good afternoon. / Good evening.

Requests

Is Helen there? May I speak to her?

May I speak to Helen please?

Farewells

Talk to you later.

I have to **hang up.**

Bye (for now).

Goodbye.

See you later.

So long.

to hang up: to end a telephone conversation.

STRATEGY

See **Pay selective attention,** p. 184.

it's raining cats and dogs.

It's raining a lot, very hard or for a long time.

A Special Toy for a Special Day 📢

A. Board Game

B. Puzzle

C. Croquet

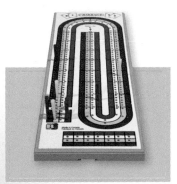

D. Cribbage Board

E. Darts

F. Skittles

G. Brain Teaser Puzzle

H. Cup and Ball Game

Activity 2

Even adults play. Your parents have their favourite games too. What if you wanted to buy them something?

1. **Listen to** the conversation between the teenager and the saleslady.

2. **Name** the games he finally chooses.

3. Have you ever seen any of these games? See **Talk About It.**

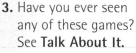

WRITE ABOUT IT!

Do you always play the same games?

Do you always call the same people?

What games do you like to play when it's raining outside?

Which of these games have you ever tried?

Did you think they were fun?

What games do your parents play?

Do you sometimes play with them?

TALK ABOUT IT!

A Video-Game Booklet

STEP 1

When you play a new video game, do you always read the instruction **booklet**?

Before Reading

1. **Look** at the titles of sections in the **booklet**.

2. How many sections are presented?

Reading

3. **Read** the sentences on page 105.

4. **Compare** how the sentences are written.

5. **Match** each sentence to the appropriate section of the **booklet**.

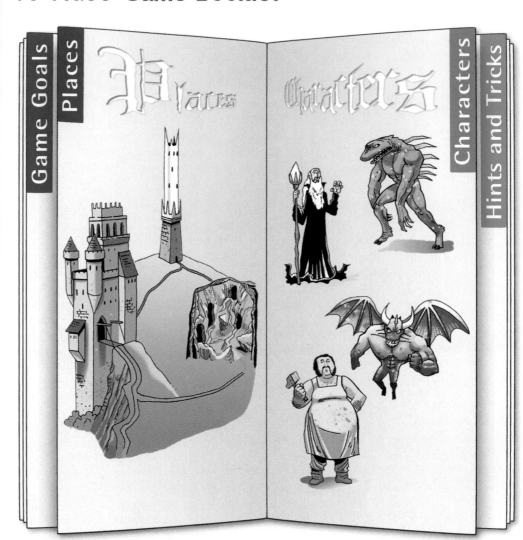

STRATEGY

See **Compare**, p. 188.

Discourse markers

First,	we will read the	name of the section.
After,		
Then,		
Finally,		

TALK
ABOUT IT!

A Citizens and priests are very helpful.

B You have to capture your enemies.

C Don't travel alone at night.

D The Tower of Light doubles the power of your character.

E Use the spacebar to trigger your action mode.

F The Green Castle is useful for getting advice.

G Follow the map to find your way.

H Wizards and fairies can heal you.

I Caverns are useful for finding magic items.

J Drink a green potion when you're low on health points.

K Blacksmiths can repair your broken armour.

L You have to free your people.

M Buy a blue gem to have more magic powers.

N Apothecaries can mix some potions for you.

O The magic key opens all the doors.

P You might want to sleep in an inn when you're tired.

Q The Dark Caves are very dangerous.

R Ghouls, demons, sorcerers and zombies are dangerous.

S You have to stop the evil demon.

▼ Reinvest

9. With a classmate, decide the order in which to read the sections of the booklet. See **Talk About It.**

Reading *(continued)*

6. Do you have enough information to understand the game?

After reading

7. What kind of video game is this?
- a space shootout
- a role-playing fantasy
- a time travel adventure
- a flight simulator

8. What keywords in the sentences helped you guess?

VOCABULARY

blacksmith:

booklet: a short manual or guide.

gem:

inn: a small hotel.

to trigger: to activate.

wizard: a magician.

Are Video and Computer Games Addictive?

A few years ago, many people accused television of being bad for children and teens. Now video and computer games are the new champions for spending time at home. Are they really bad or even dangerous?

Some facts and numbers

Video and computer games of the 21st century are more diverse and interesting than ever. They offer players more **rewards** and challenge. Now, young children are attracted to video games around 4 years old. Most teens over 11 years old play video or computer games daily.

- 7% of these teens play more than 30 hours/ week;
- More than 25% play around 20 hours/week.

What's the problem?

Gamers, good players or addicted players will play for long periods, sometimes over 5 hours in a **row**. They develop headaches, sore eyes and stomach aches. They don't know how to stop. They become obsessed by the game.

Some people are asking for a **ban** on video and computer games. Is this the only thing to do?

CULTURE

Video and computer games are becoming the #1 entertainment industry, even bigger than the movie industry. Now video games have a rating system just like movies.

Questionnaire

How do you know if you're a game addict?

A Do you play almost every day?

B Do you often play for long periods? (Over 3-4 hours at a time?)

C Do you play mainly for the **thrill**?

D Do you get nervous and irritable if you can't play?

E Do you choose to play instead of seeing friends?

F Do you play instead of doing homework?

G Can you control your reflex to play?

> If you answered "yes" to four or more questions, you might be playing too much.

Reading *(continued)*

4. **Answer** the questionnaire of the article.

5. How many "yes" answers do you have?

6. **Read** the solutions.

After reading

7. Are you a game addict or do you feel someone you know may be a game addict?

8. Are the solutions in the text interesting?

9. Do you agree with the solutions?

What are the solutions?

1. Try more strategy games rather than highly violent ones.

2. Play with friends instead of alone. Make your games a social activity.

3. Set yourself a 1-hour time limit when playing.

4. Stop for at least 15 minutes every hour when you play.

5. Get up, stretch, walk around and get your body moving. Don't forget to eat and drink!

Conclusion

One thing is for sure: if you don't want to become a game zombie, you need to set yourself some limits.

> That's the smartest dog I've ever seen.

> Nah, he's not so smart, he only beat me once.

▼ Reinvest

What do think about all that? Do you have the feeling you play too much?

10. **Compare** your results with your classmates.

11. **Tell** them your opinion about video and computer gaming.

Gabrielle Dacost 1c

See **Encourage self and others,** p. 196.

STEP 3

Some games you know might be a lot older than you think.

Before reading

1. Do you know any games that are very ancient?

2. **Team up** with one or three classmates.

Reading

3. **Use** the handouts to prepare your game board.

4. **Read** the rules of the game.

After reading

5. Do you know a game that looks like this one?

6. Do you remember its name?

STRATEGY

Pachisi

Rules of Pachisi

What you need (material):

- A board (on the handout)
- 6 identical coins
- 16 **pawns** – 4 coloured **pawns**/player

Players:

- Two or four players.
- For two players, each one takes two opposite teams of **pawns**.

How to win:

To win, players have to move all their **pawns** around the board and bring them into the "Charkoni."

Getting started:

Players place their pawns in the "Charkoni".

Each player throws the coins once. The coins will fall on either heads or tails. To see your score, look at the Scoring Table. The highest score starts the game.

Scoring Table

When you throw	Your score is
	**2** Move 2 squares.
	**3** Move 3 squares.
	**4** Move 4 squares.
	**5** Move 5 squares.
	**6** Move 6 squares + play again.
	**10** Move 10 squares + play again.
	**25** Move 25 squares + play again.

Anaelle Paradis 1A

Playing the game:

To get out of the Charkoni, you must get 6, 10 or 25 when you throw the coins.

Move your pawns around the board by throwing the coins. Follow the arrows.

The black squares on the board are called "castles."

You can have pawns of the same team on the same square, but only one on the castle.

If your pawn ends up on a square where there is already another team's pawn(s), you "eat" it or them. The other team's pawns are sent back to the Charkoni and have to start again. After placing them in the Charkoni, play your own pawn again.

You cannot "eat" another pawn on a castle.

When a pawn finally arrives back in the Charkoni, lay it down on its side.

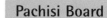

Pachisi Board

CHARKONI

▼ **Reinvest**

7. Play a Pachisi game.
8. Who won the game?

Use these expressions to get your game going.

It's your turn.

Good move!

Lucky shot!

Watch out!

Whose turn is it?

Throw the coins.

What a move!

Nice one!

Be careful.

You got me!

TALK ABOUT IT!

Project A
Getting Started

Different people have different reasons, places and moments to play games.

Before reading

1. **Look at** the questions.

2. What kind of information is each question asking for?
   - time;
   - place;
   - games;
   - persons;
   - reasons;
   - amount of time.

Reading

3. **Read** the questions and the choice of answers.

v o c A b u L a r y

stuffed animal:

Interviews About Gaming

Who do you play with?

I play alone.

I play with my family.

I play with my friends.

When do you play?

I play on weekends only.

I play all the time.

I play in the evenings, after my homework is done.

Where do you play?

I play on the kitchen table.

I play with the TV in the living room.

I play outside because there's more room.

What games do you play?

I play board games and card games.

I play with my dolls and **stuffed animals**.

I play video games.

 Why do you play?

I play because it helps me relax.

I play to enjoy myself.

I play because I like competition.

Reading (continued)

4. Ask three classmates these questions.

After Reading

5. What would your answers be?

When is it dangerous to play cards?

When the jokers are wild!

 How much time per week do you play?

I play about 5 hours per week.

I play about 15 hours per week.

I play more than 25 hours a week!

▼ Reinvest

A Game Survey   PROJECT A

Now it is time to go out and ask people questions about their gaming habits.

Don't forget to include in your project:
- General questions as well as specific questions;
- Questions applicable to people of all ages;
- Questions that ask about places, game types, time spent, reasons, goals, etc.

How Old Are Your Games?

Project B
Getting Started

Some of the games we play have been around for a very long time. See for yourself.

Before Reading

1. **Skim** the timeline.

2. **Look at** the colour key.

| Red = Toys |
| Purple = Games for everyone |
| Green = Video games |

Reading

3. **Read** the information on the timeline.

4. **Answer** the questions on your handout.

Dice in use in Egypt.
±6000 B.C.

Games related to **Chess** and **Checkers** played in Babylon.
4000 B.C.

Egyptians play **checkers** with **stone marbles**.
2000 B.C.

3000 B.C.
Backgammon is played in Ancient Sumeria.

1000 B.C.
Egyptians play with **hula hoops** and **stone yo-yos** are found in Greece.

| PREHISTORY | ANTIQUITY | | MIDDLE AGES |
| 5,000,000 B.C. | 3500 B.C. | 476 B.C. | |

The first **roller-skates** get rolling in Scandinavia.
200

An Indian game called **Chaturanga** evolves to what will become chess.
600

300
Pachisi played in India.

1000
Playing cards are used in parts of Asia.

STRATEGY

See **Skim**, p. 192.

VOCABULARY

B. C.: abbreviation of Before Christ.

dice:

die:

CULTURE

The creators of the teddy bear were inspired by the story of the former U.S. President, Theodore Roosevelt, who refused to shoot a bear cub. They named the stuffed animal "Teddy".

Ludo, a Western version of **Pachisi**, comes out in England.
1896

Dominoes are invented in China.
1100

Dolls are mass-produced in America.
1840

The teddy bear is born.
1902

1300
Playing cards are introduced in Europe.

1901
The **toy train** is introduced.

●●●●●●●●●●●●●●●●●

After reading

5. What is the difference between a toy and a game?

6. Which games and toys have you played with?

7. Do you have any favourites that are not on the timeline? **Name** them.

RENAISSANCE	REVOLUTION ERA	TWENTIETH CENTURY ▶
1700	1880	1995

The **yo-yo** becomes very popular in America.
1929

A Danish man comes up with new building blocks: **Lego**.
1949

Monopoly is finally commercialized by Parker Brothers.
1936

The **G.I. Joe doll** is a great success... for boys!
1969

Video games get a rating system.
1993

1931
A new word game is introduced: Scrabble.

1930s
Kids build themselves skateboards.

1943
Slinky, the walking spring, is invented.

1959
Say hello to the **Barbie doll**.

1975
The first popular home video game "**Pong**" is released.

Reinvest

History of a Game

PROJECT B

Choose any of the games or toys found on the timeline or another one that your teacher accepts and tell us more about it.

Don't forget to:
- Explain where it comes from.
- Say how old it is.
- Explain the game: How do we play the game? How many players do we need? How long does it take to play?

Let's Play!

Luke

Ally

Brenda

Aston

●●●●●●●●●●●●●●●●●

Project C
Getting Started

What kind of player are you? A fair player? A bad loser?

Before Reading

1. **Skim** the comic strip.

2. What is the strip about?

Reading

3. **Read** the dialogue.

4. Identify each player's type.
   - **fair play;**
   - sore loser
   - bad loser;
   - pessimist;
   - optimist;
   - aggressive;
   - patient;
   - impatient.

After reading

5. How would you have reacted?

6. Do you think Brenda was right at the end?

7. What type of player are you?

CULTURE

Fair play allows everybody to enjoy a game. It is not a sign of weakness. It is particularly important in certain cultures such as the English culture.

▼ **Reinvest**

A Game Tournament   **PROJECT C**

It's time to organise your tournament. Don't forget to include:
- The rules of participation for the tournament;
- The registration board and the schedule.

Your Project Presentation

- Did you work individually or in a team?

- Was it clear what you had to do for each task? Was it the same for your teammates?

- How much time did you spend on your project?

- How will the audience participate during your presentation?

- Do you have all the material you need?

- Are you prepared to interact with the audience or the participants?

- Do you need more pratice before showing your work?

It's time to present your project.

Focus on the most important elements in order to make it more interesting.

Your Portfolio

During this unit, you experienced a lot of different activities related to games and gaming. You learned to use some new words and expressions; you learned to use new strategies when interacting orally, or reading and listening to texts.

Be sure to put the following items in your portfolio:

- The *In this Unit* handout, to self-evaluate your learning in relation to oral interaction and strategies.

- All the notes and short texts you wrote in the Reinvest section at the end of some of the activities.

- The *Vocabulary* and *Language* handouts that you completed.

- The *Evaluation* handouts you completed.

- Any texts, documents or pictures that can help you present your project.

TV Time

1. Look at the TV screens.

2. Match each kind of program to the appropriate screen.

3. What kind of TV programs do you prefer?

Kinds of TV programs

SPORTS

CARTOONS

DOCUMENTARIES

TALK SHOWS

MUSIC VIDEOS

GAME SHOWS

SITCOMS

IN THIS UNIT

You Will...

- think about the good and bad aspects of TV viewing;
- identify your profile as a TV viewer;
- find out about TV history;
- learn about the Canadian Television Classification System.

Text types

Look at, read and/or listen to...

a survey, a questionnaire, a time-line, emails, a teen magazine article, symbols, comic strips.

Key elements of advertisements: photos and slogans.

Strategies

- pay selective attention;
- infer with cognates;
- scan.

Projects

Write or produce one of the following projects:

- *A TV Survey;*
- *A TV Commercial;*
- *A Review of a TV Program.*

Quick TV Survey

Activity 1

What kind of TV programs do you watch? What do your classmates watch? Complete the survey and find out.

1. **Read** the survey.

2. **Ask** your classmates about their TV viewing habits. See **Talk About It.**

3. **Write down** the names of the persons.

4. **Share** the results with your classmates.

Find someone who...

A) ... watched an action movie on TV last weekend.

B) ... watches sports on TV occasionally.

C) ... did not watch television yesterday.

D) ... never watches television in English.

E) ... watched television in English last week.

F) ... watches television in the bedroom.

G) ... likes documentaries.

H) ... does homework in front of the television.

I) ... likes soap operas and reality shows.

J) ... enjoys watching TV ads.

VOCABULARY

ads: (abbreviation of advertisement): commercials.

Idiom

lazybones: an inactive person, someone who sits or lies down a lot.

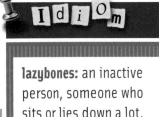

Present		Past	
Do you	watch...?	Did you	watch...?
	like...?		
	enjoy...?		
	do...?		

TALK ABOUT IT!

TV Zapping 🔊

EDWARD ▶
SUZIE ▼
JASON

①

② Kiddy Land

③ SCARY HARRY

④ MAX, TIM AND FRIENDS

⑤ THE ROBOT MISSION

⑥ Bobby the Dog

⑦ TEEN MAG

⑧ CLICK!

CULTURE

Activity 2 📝

Do you always agree about what to watch on TV? Who usually takes control of the TV zapper at home?

1. **Listen** to the conversation.

2. Which programs would Suzie like to see?

3. Which programs would Edward like to see?

4. Which programs would Jason like to see?

5. Which of these programs would you have chosen?

STRATEGY

See **Pay selective attention,** p. 184.

TV Habits

STEP 1

What are your TV viewing habits? Are you a passionate, indifferent, or occasional TV viewer?

Before listening

1. **Look at** the pictures.

2. Which of these teenagers have bad TV viewing habits?

Listening

3. **Listen** to the teenagers.

4. **Find out** who is talking.

After listening

5. What type of TV viewer are you? Are you more like Luke, Selma, Tess or Calvin?

A)

C)

B)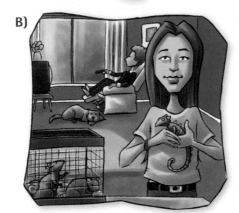

D)

Idiom

couch potato

▼ **Reinvest**

6. Complete the handout on your TV habits.

Some Facts About TV

In London, England, **John Logie Baird** develops and creates the first television studios. He transmits a television signal between London and New York, but produces only jerky images.
1924–1929

In **Montreal**, VE9EC is Canada's first TV station (it was created by *CKAC* and *La Presse*).
1931

There are about 100 million black and white TV sets in use around the world.
1960

There are over one billion TV sets in use around the world.
1996

??
1950-1960

There are only 2,000 TV sets in use around the world.
1936

Canadian stations transmit colour television signals for the first time.
1966

1928
W2XBS, the first New York TV station creates **Felix the Cat**, the first *TV star*.

1939
A baseball game is televised for the first time.

1952
??

TV sets are manufactured in Canada. With the opening of TV stations in big cities, TV audiences increase 4,000 percent in only one year.
1948

1979
??

1975
Studies show that by age 75, the average person will have spent nearly 10 full years of his/her life in front of a TV set.

1927
In England, the **BBC** (British Broadcasting Corporation) and in the U.S., the **CBS** (Columbia Broadcasting System) are formed.

1969
??

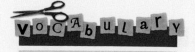

Statements

A) There are about 300 million TV sets in use around the world.

B) Like radio shows, TV programs are transmitted "live", but only for a few hours each day.

C) CBC (Canadian Broadcasting Corporation) Television and Radio Canada start transmitting in both languages, English and French.

D) On July 20, 19??, 600 million people watch the first live TV transmission from the Moon. Some TV stations transmit 24 hours a day.

STEP 2

Do you know that TV is almost 80 years old? What do you know about TV history?

Before reading

1. **Look at** the timeline and this colour key.

   Special facts
   Inventions
   Audience

2. Of the three, what type of information do you find the most interesting?

Reading

3. **Read** the timeline.

4. **Match** each of the four statements with the correct date.

After reading

5. What information on the timeline do you find the most surprising?

vocabulary

jerky: unclear, stopping and starting.

▼ Reinvest

6. **Add** three new facts to this timeline obtained from books, the Internet or your personal knowledge.

Your TV Viewer Profile

STEP 3

How much time do you spend watching TV? Do you plan your TV viewing?

Before reading

1. **Look at** the pictures on this page.

2. **In your opinion**, are these habits good or not?

Reading

3. **Read** the questions carefully.

4. **Answer** each question honestly. Use *sometimes*, *never* or *always* in your answers.

5. **Write down** your answers in your notebook.

STRATEGY

See **Infer with cognates**, p. 190.

Questions

A) Do you do your homework in front of the television?

B) Do you interrupt all your activities to watch your favourite TV programs?

C) Do you spend your free time in front of the TV?

D) During weeknights, do you prefer watching TV instead of practicing a sport or reading?

E) Do you watch TV because you don't know what to do?

F) Do you watch TV while eating?

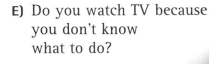

What does Batman's mom say when she wants him to come for dinner?

"Dinner, dinner, dinner, DInner, dinner, DInner, dinner, Batmaaaaaaaaan!"

Profile Interpretation

■ **Did you answer "always" to question B or D?**

You are a passionate TV viewer.

Be careful! Television can be a great learning tool. However, television is not reality. Talk about and discuss the TV shows with your parents and friends. Don't forget that real people are more precious than your favourite TV heroes and idols.

■ **Did you answer "always" to question A or F?**

You are probably a wallpaper TV viewer.

You certainly can do many things at the same time! That's excellent! However, don't let television dominate your family life. Try a few moments of silence once in a while; it is very refreshing.

■ **Did you answer "always" to question C or E?**

You are a fill-in-time TV viewer.

Why don't you try a new hobby? Why don't you practice a sport? Be more creative. There are so many ways to enjoy life.

▼ **Reinvest**

9. **Ask** your classmates what their TV viewer's profile is. See Talk About It.

After Reading

6. **Look at** your answers.

   If you did not answer **always,** it means that your profile is a happy mix.

7. **Read** the profiles of the three TV viewers on this page.

8. Which one is similar to your TV viewer profile?

once in a while: sometimes, not very often.

tool: any instrument used for doing a job.

wallpaper TV viewer: a person who lives with TV as a background to other activities.

1. What is your TV viewer's profile?

2. How many hours do you spend watching TV a night?

3. Do you think it's too much, or too little?

4. How many hours per week do you consider acceptable?

5. What other activities could replace television? (Name at least three.)

TALK ABOUT IT!

Reader's Corner

TV Matters

Did you know that TV stations have rules to follow? Do you know where to complain when you see things you don't like on TV?

Before Reading

1. **Look at** the title of this section.

2. What is the significa- tion of "matters"?

3. **Name** one thing you don't like to see on TV.

Reading

4. **Read** these two letters.

5. **Note** what each per- son is complaining about.

6. Do you agree with the opinions expressed in the letters?

Dear Editor,

My letter is about ethnic stereotyping on TV. I love watching TV. I espe- cially like comedies and dramas. However, I often don't like the representation of ethnic groups on TV. They are often ridiculed in comedies, and they are associated with criminals in dramas. They are too often **pictured** as poor or uneducated people.

In my opinion, TV shows should not **perpetuate** prejudices. TV programs should show more respect for ethnic diversity, as in real life.

Thank you for reading my letter.

Jessica Cormier
14 years old
Moncton, New Brunswick

Dear Editor,

I feel very concerned about all the violence and bad language on TV. Violence has increased dramatically on TV in Canada the last few years. This physical violence often appears before 9 p.m. At this time many young people are still watching.

Young children are easily influenced. They are often alone in front of the TV set with no one to tell them that violence and bad lan- guage is not acceptable.

I wish that there were less violence on the **tube**. I think that TV stations should be more responsible and respectful of their young audience.

Liam Davis
15 years old
Calgary, Alberta

to perpetuate: to continue something indefinitely.

to picture: to represent, to describe, to show.

tube: television.

Audience Classification Symbols

Descriptions

7. Read the six descriptions on this page.

8. Match the letter of each description to the correct symbol.

A) These programs are acceptable for all ages. They may contain minimal violence.

B) These programs are for all children. There is no realistic violence, no offensive language, no nudity.

C) These programs are not for children under 8 years old. Parents should supervise viewing for 8 to 13-year-old children.

D) These programs are for 18 years or older. Themes are not intended for children. They may contain violence, bad language and nudity.

E) These programs are for children 8 years or older. Parents should watch these shows with their children.

F) These programs are for 14 years or older. Parents should not let younger children view these programs. They may contain intense violence, frequent use of bad language and nudity.

▼ Reinvest

9. **Name** your Top-5 favourite TV programs.

10. **Guess** which classifications they have.

11. **Check** in a TV schedule or in the Internet to see if your guesses about the classifications are correct.

STRATEGY

See **Scan**, p. 192.

Television and You

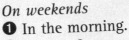

Project A
Getting Started

Almost everyone watches TV. Are we all TV addicts?

Before reading

1. **Look at** the survey.

2. What kind of information will you **gather** with this survey?
   • TV viewing habits;
   • favourite TV programs;
   • favourite TV **schedule**.

Reading

3. **Team up** with a classmate.

4. **Read** the survey.

5. **Answer** the questions in a notebook.

data: information.

to gather: to collect.

relevant: important, interesting, appropriate.

schedule: a plan or list of events over time (during a day, a week, a month, etc.).

A. When do you usually watch TV?

On weekdays
❶ In the morning, before going to school.
❷ At lunchtime.
❸ After school.
❹ In the evening, after dinner.
❺ Before going to bed.

On weekends
❶ In the morning.
❷ In the afternoon.
❸ In the evening.

B. Where do you usually watch TV?
❶ In your room.
❷ In the family room or living room.
❸ In the kitchen.
❹ In the bathroom.

C. With whom do you usually watch TV?
❶ With your family members.
❷ No one.
❸ With your friends.

D. Why do you usually watch TV?
❶ Because I have nothing to do.
❷ Because I don't know what to do.
❸ Because I want to see a specific program I like.
❹ Because I feel like being alone in my room.

E. Do you usually watch TV when...
❶ ... you eat breakfast, lunch or dinner?
❷ ... you do your homework?
❸ ... you spend time with your friends?
❹ ... you are alone.

F. How many TV sets do you have at home?
❶ None.
❷ One.
❸ Two or three.
❹ Four or more.

G. What is your favourite kind of TV program?
- ❶ Sports.
- ❷ Documentaries.
- ❸ Sitcoms.
- ❹ Cartoons.
- ❺ Music videos.
- ❻ Movies on TV (not DVD or VHS).

H. How many hours per week do you spend watching TV?
- ❶ 6 hours a week or less.
- ❷ Between 6 and 12 hours a week.
- ❸ Between 12 and 20 hours a week.
- ❹ More than 20 hours a week.

I. Do your parents limit your TV viewing time?
- ❶ Yes.
- ❷ No.
- ❸ Sometimes.

J. How many hours per week do you spend in front of a screen?
(this includes watching TV, watching DVDs, playing computer games or using game consoles)

- ❶ 6 hours a week or less.
- ❷ Between 6 and 12 hours a week.
- ❸ Between 12 and 20 hours a week.
- ❹ Between 20 and 30 hours a week.
- ❺ More than 30 hours a week.

After Reading

6. Looking at your answers, do you think you watch too much television? If yes, what else could you do to spend your free time?

▼ **Reinvest**

A TV Survey   **PROJECT A**

When you carry out your project:
- Try to interview your family members and your friends;
- Ask them to answer your questions honestly;
- Interpret your results using only the most **relevant data**.

Between Commercials and Reality

Project B
Getting Started

Do you like TV commercials? Do you think ads are realistic? Do you think commercials make people buy things because they see them on TV?

Before Reading

1. **Look at** the titles of each of the commercials on pages 128 and 129.

2. What is this type of title called?
   - a slogan;
   - an ad.

Reading

3. **Read** the commercials.

4. **Find** one commercial that does not make sense.

mess: something disordered, untidy.

parody: a funny imitation.

ratings: estimation of the number of people that watch or listen to a TV show, a radio program, etc.

to train: to get ready for a sports event by repeated practice.

COMMERCIAL 1 *Pink Essence Shampoo: It's dab-e-di-dew!*

"My hair is fabulous, isn't it?"

"But mine is a **mess**! I look awful, don't you think?"

"Pink Essence makes my hair soft and silky."

"Why don't you try Pink Essence? Make your life dab-e-di-dew!"

COMMERCIAL 2 Kamata Fury! There is electricity in the air!

"No, thank you. I don't need any gas today! I'm electric, but you can wash my windows."

"I feel free in my Kamata Fury. Electricity works for me."

"I hate those new cars!"

There is electricty in the air!

COMMERCIAL **3** *In shape with Mega's burgers!*

"Hi! I'm Mickael Peters. To be an Olympic champion, I have to **train** hard everyday."

"After training, I deserve the best. This is why I choose Mega's burgers. Mmmmm yummy! "

"Don't you deserve the best at the best price? Hurry! This offer is for a limited time only. Get in shape with Mega's burgers!"

Reading

5. **Team up** with a classmate.

6. **Practise** and **present** one commercial to the class.

After reading

7. In your opinion, which of these commercials is the best one?

8. Some people want TV to be free of commercials. Do you think it is a good idea?

CULTURE

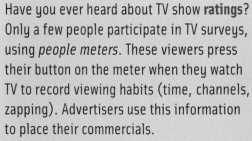

Have you ever heard about TV show **ratings**? Only a few people participate in TV surveys, using *people meters*. These viewers press their button on the meter when they watch TV to record viewing habits (time, channels, zapping). Advertisers use this information to place their commercials.

▼ **Reinvest**

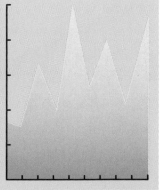

PROJECT B

A TV Commercial

When you plan your project and practice your **parody**:

• Take note of some of the slogans in the commercials you see;

• Take note of the stereotypes and nonsense you see;

• Make a list of slogans, then modify and imitate them.

Project C
Getting Started

Watching TV in English can help you learn the language. Do you ever watch TV programs in English? Which one is your favourite?

Before reading

1. **Look at** this questionnaire that Gwen has filled in.

Reading

2. **Read** the questions and answers.

3. **Fill in** your handout.

After reading

4. Do you think you would have like Gwen's favourite TV program?

▼ **Reinvest**

PROJECT C

A TV Program Review

In presenting your favourite program, don't forget to include:
• the title, the kind and the time;
• a short program description.

Viewing Frequency

How much television did you watch in English this week?

I watched a total of 6 1/2 hours of television in English.

TV Programs Viewed

What TV programs did you watch?

I watched The Weather News, The Johnsons, The Scary Gang and a movie titled The X-Mission with my brother.

Favourite TV Program

What was your favourite English-language television program?

The Scary Gang was my favourite program.

Channel, Day and Time

On what channel does it play? On which day and at what time is it on?

It plays on channel 12, every weekday at 4 p.m.

Audience

For which audience was it intended? (see page 125)

It was intended for all audiences.

Kind of Program

What was the kind of program? (documentary, adventure series, sitcom, talk show, game show, cartoon, children's show, science-fiction series, comedy)

It was a cartoon.

Short Program Description

What was it about? Who were the main characters? Who was the host of the show?

It was about a group of friends who work together to solve mysteries.
The main characters are two girls, two boys and a cat. There wasn't a host.

Your Rating

Give a rating to your TV show.

★ boring   ★ ★ good    ★ ★ ★ very good   ★ ★ ★ ★ excellent

Your Project Presentation

- Did you work individually or in a team?

- Did you complete each task you had to do?

- How much time did you spend on your project?

- If you produced the TV Survey or reviewed a TV program, how will you present your results? Which items will interest your audience the most?

- If you produced a TV commercial, did you tape it or will you present it as a skit in front of the class?

- Do you need more practice before showing your project?

It's time to present your project.

Plan your presentation so it will captivate your audience right from the start.

Your Portfolio

During this unit, you reflected and expressed your opinions on issues and subjects related to TV viewing and content. You learned to use some new words and expressions; you learned to use new strategies when interacting orally, and reading or listening to texts.

Be sure to put the following items in your portfolio:

- The *In this Unit* handout, to self-evaluate your learning in relation to oral interactions, texts and strategies.

- All the notes and short texts you wrote in the Reinvest section at the end of some of the activities.

- The *Vocabulary* and *Language* handouts that you completed.

- The *Evaluation* handouts you completed.

- Any texts, documents or pictures that can help you present your project.

JUPITER

MARS

SATURN

EARTH

URANUS

NEPTUNE

PLUTO

Match each riddle with the name of a planet.

A) I was named in honour of the master of the Roman gods.

B) I am the brightest planet in the sky at night.

C) I am the closest planet to the Sun.

D) I probably like jewellery since I have many rings.

E) So far, I am the only one with living creatures and I look like a big blue marble.

VENUS

MERCURY

IN THIS UNIT
You Will...

- learn about planets and mythology;
- read texts about space facts and science fiction;
- learn about the history of space exploration;
- discover a special message in a bottle;
- reflect on space exploration in the future.

Text Types

Look at, read and/or listen to...
  riddles, comic strips, letters, a questionnaire, a timeline, myths, magazine articles, encyclopedia articles, advertisements.

Key elements of:
  short stories – characters
  advertisements – slogans.

Strategies

- predict with pictures;
- skim;
- scan;
- infer with cognates and visual clues.

Projects

Write or produce one of the following projects:

- *A Space Trip Ad;*
- *A Space Story;*
- *A Space Travel Timeline.*

F) I am the farthest planet from the Sun.

G) Although I was named after the Roman god of the seas, I have no water.

H) My nickname is the Red Planet even if my inhabitants were thought to be green.

I) I am the third largest planet in the solar system.

Planets and Mythology... Who's Who?

Activity 1

How much do you know about the planets? Do you know some gods and goddesses of Antiquity?

1. **Look at** the illustrations on this page.

2. **Read** the texts.

3. **Read** the **Word Bank**.

4. **Find** the name of each god or goddess related to the solar system planets (see also pages 132-133).

STRATEGY

See **Predict** with pictures, p. 187.

I n Roman mythology, I am the master of Olympus and the patron of Rome. In 1610, Galileo discovered my four large moons – Io, Europa, Ganymede and Callisto – the Galilean moons. The planet probably received my name because it is the biggest in the solar system.

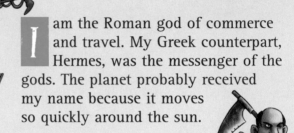

I am the Roman god of commerce and travel. My Greek counterpart, Hermes, was the messenger of the gods. The planet probably received my name because it moves so quickly around the sun.

I am the Roman god of agriculture. Galileo was the first to observe my rings with a telescope. I have 32 moons; the last two were discovered in 2003 and 2004.

I am the Roman god of the dead. The planet discovered in 1930 was so named because it is so far from the Sun that it seems to be in perpetual darkness.

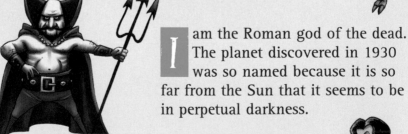

I am the Roman goddess of love and beauty. The planet was so named probably because it is the brightest object in the sky except for the Sun and the Moon.

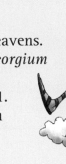

I am the ancient Greek god of the heavens. William Herschel, who named it *Georgium Sidus* in honor of the English king George III, discovered the planet in 1781. My name was proposed in 1850 to fit in better with the mythological origins of the others.

5. a) **Find out** which five planets were known in Antiquity.

b) **Which** sentences in the text help you find the five planets?

I am the Roman god of war. The planet probably received my name because of its red colour. It has two moons: Deimos and Phobos named after the sons of Ares, my Greek counterpart.

I am the Roman god of the sea. Two astronomers, Galle and d'Arrest, discovered the planet in 1845. It has 13 moons, 4 of which were discovered in 2002 and one in 2003.

word bank

Mercury

Venus

Earth

Mars

Jupiter

Saturn

Uranus

Neptune

Pluto

CULTURE

The word ***planet*** comes from the ancient Greek *planêtês* which means "traveller". That is because people looked at stars and could see some of them changing positions. In Antiquity, people knew about only five planets and named them after their gods, Roman or Greek.

In 2003, a small object was discovered beyond the orbit of Pluto. It was named SEDNA and is a bit smaller than Pluto. Some people think it is the tenth planet of our solar system, but it is too small to qualify as a planet.

Here is a helper to remember the names and the order of the planets:

My **V**ery **E**xcellent
Mother **J**ust **S**ent **U**s
Nine **P**izzas

Facts About Space and Science Fiction

Activity 2

Fact or fiction? real or unreal? True or false? Don't confuse science with science fiction.

1. **Read** the articles.

2. On your handout, **find** the keywords of each article.

3. **Decide** if each article is fact or fiction.

4. **Compare** your answers with a classmate.

VOCABULARY

due to: because of.

dust: small particles of matter or loose earth.

novel: a fictional story written in a book.

novelist: a person who writes novels (a story in a book).

space probe: a device used to explore space.

through: from one side to the other.

to wash away: to remove, to efface.

A) Sometimes, the moon looks blue. Scientists believe this is caused by **dust** in Earth's atmosphere that only lets blue light come through.

B) In the 1950s, scientist and science fiction novelist Isaac Asimov created a device he called a *positronic* brain. It is used on all robots today.

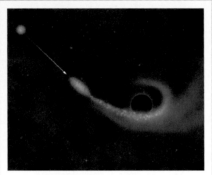

C) A black hole has such strong gravity that even light cannot escape from it. That is why it is black.

D) The Voyager I space probe is ready to meet aliens. It carries a disk on board telling aliens who and where we are.

EARTH

EARTH'S TWIN PLANET

E) A real twin planet of Earth circles the sun on its opposite side. That is why we can never see it.

F) The existence of the Perseids meteor shower is due to the Earth passing through the debris of comets.

G) Rainbows can occur at night. They are called "moonbows". Next time you see bright moonlight shining down on falling water, look closely and you might see one.

H) What sounds can we hear in space? None. Sound needs solid, liquid or gaseous matter in order to travel (to vibrate). Space is silent.

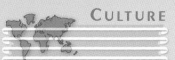

On July 22, 1969, the astronaut Neil Armstrong was the first man to walk on the Moon. His famous quote: *That's one small step for a man, one giant leap for mankind.*

I) Jules Verne, in his 1865 novel *From Earth to the Moon*, predicted that man would one day walk on the moon.

L) The footprints left on the moon by the astronauts are still there. This is because there is no wind or water to blow or wash them away.

K) The temperature on the Moon is 120°C in the day and −170°C at night.

J) The Apollo 13 mission to the moon was almost a disaster. This mission left Earth on April 11, 1970 at 2:13 p.m., Eastern Standard Time.

STEP 1

How much do you know about outer space? Do you know the name of each of the objects found in space?

Before reading

1. **Look at** the statements on this page.

2. What type of statements are they?
   • information;
   • questions;
   • parts of definitions.

Reading

3. **Read** the statements.

4. **Match** each statement with one of the words in the **Word Bank**.

STRATEGY

See **Skim**, p. 192.

CULTURE

A meteorite entering Earth's atmosphere is often called a *shooting star.*

The Recruiting Test

HA

Humanity Spatial Agency
HSA Headquarters, 123, Space St, Earth, Solar System

A) The biggest planet in our solar system.

B) This celestial object looks like a giant dirty snowball.

C) These are pieces of rock falling from the sky. The largest number of them can be seen around mid-August every year.

D) These objects are more dangerous than meteors if they encounter a planet.

E) It is a theory about a big blast that created the universe.

F) This is a gigantic hole in space. Anything getting close to it is pulled in right away.

G) Its speed of 300,000 m/s makes it the fastest phenomenon in the universe.

H) It is a flat disk about 100,000 light years in diameter and 5,000 light years thick. It is composed of stars and stellar dust.

I) Our sun is not the largest. It is only a medium-sized one.

J) This is a natural satellite that orbits around a planet.

CONFIDENTIAL

word bank

comet

moon

black hole

asteroid

Milky Way

star

meteorite

Big Bang

star light

Jupiter

Test Interpretation

10 correct answers:
Great for a recruit! You are ready to go into astronaut training.

7 to 9 correct answers:
Not bad for a recruit, but you will have to study a little bit more.

4 to 6 correct answers:
Don't feel bad. It was a nice try anyway.

Less than 5 correct answers:
Hey! Some of us have to stay behind and applaud.

Reading *(continued)*

5. Ask your teacher for the answer key and **interpret** your results.

After reading

6. Did you know all the celestial objects described by the statements?

7. Which do you find the most fascinating?

STRATEGY

See **Scan**, p. 192.

VOCABULARY

celestial: of the sky.

to pull in: to attract.

recruit: a new member of a group.

▼ Reinvest

8. Scan the statements to find comparatives and superlatives.

WRITE ABOUT IT!

You can describe people, animals or things using comparatives or superlatives.

Comparatives

These objects are **more dangerous than** meteors.
The Sun is **bigger than** Jupiter.

Superlatives

Mercury is the **most dangerous** planet in the solar system.
Jupiter is **the biggest** planet in the solar system.

STEP 2

For centuries, mankind has dreamed of flying. Do you know the events and inventions that made it possible?

Before reading and listening

1. **Skim** the chapters in the text on pages 140 to 143.

2. What is the structure of those chapters?
   - chronological order;
   - subject order;
   - both.

Reading and listening

3. **Read** and **listen to** each chapter.

4. In your notebook, **write** a title for each chapter. ◄■■■►

STRATEGY

See **Infer with cognates and visual clues**, p. 190-191.

From *Kitty Hawk* to the Future 📢

Chapter I

In 1903, two brothers named Wilbur and Orville Wright opened the modern era of flying at Kitty Hawk, North Carolina, USA. They used a motor with **propellers** to take off from the ground. It was the birth of the **propeller** airplane. People before them flew only in balloons and **gliders**.

Unfortunately, like some inventions intended for the progress of civilization, the plane was adapted for war. During the First World War (1914-18) one- and two-seater airplanes were used to do battle in the sky. At the end of World War II (1939-45), the German engineer Messerschmitt replaced the **propellers** with a jet **engine**. The modern jet aircraft was born.

WRIGHT'S BROTHERS AIRPLANE

Chapter II

Also during the Second World War, German engineers invented the first rockets. *V1* and *V2* rockets were used to carry bombs. After the war, the same scientists turned their attention to the **heavens**.

In 1957, the first man-made object circled the Earth. It was named *Sputnik*. Later that same year, the Soviets sent *Sputnik 2* into space, together with a special passenger: a dog named Laika. The Americans founded NASA in 1958 and sent the space probe *Pioneer 1* into space.

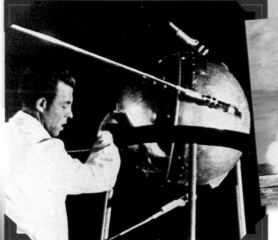

SPUTNIK

A ROCKET

The Huntsville Times

Man Enters Space

'So Close, Yet So Far,' Sighs Cape
U.S. Had Hoped For Own Launch

Soviet Officer Orbits Globe In 5-Ton Ship
Maximum Height Reached Reported As 188 Miles

Hobbs Admits 1944 Slaying

To Keep Up, U.S.A. Must Run Like Hell

Praise Is Heaped On Major Gagarin
First Man To Enter Space Is 27, Married, Father Of Two

'Worker' Stands By Story

Reds Deny Spacemen Hero Died

No Astronaut Signal Received At Ft. Monmouth

engine: a motor.

glider: an airplane that flies without using a motor.

heavens: the sky, space.

propeller:
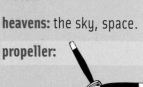

Chapter III

Then the real race for space began. Who would be first: the Soviets or the Americans. In 1961, the Soviets sent the first human being into space. Yuri Gagarin was the first man to orbit the Earth on board *Vostok 1*.

The same year, Alan B. Shepard was the first American to go into space, but his *Freedom 7* capsule did not orbit the Earth. His companion John Glenn orbited the Earth a year later. Also in 1962, the Soviet Valentina Tereshkova was the first woman in space.

Three years later, Soviets were the first to walk in space. The Americans repeated the exploit a few months later. Where would this race ever end?

ALAN B. SHEPARD

CULTURE

Americans who go into space are called astronauts and their Russian counterparts are called cosmonauts. All of them are spationauts.

In October 1998, the first American to orbit the Earth in the early 60s returned to space at the age of 77 aboard the shuttle *Discovery*. This made John Glenn the oldest person to travel in space.

JOHN GLENN

VALENTINA TERESHKOVA

*C*hapter IV

July 20, 1969. Americans Neil Armstrong and Buzz Aldrin left the lunar module *Eagle* and walked on the Moon, in the Sea of Tranquility. The *Apollo* missions sent 12 men to the Moon between 1969 and 1972. As for the Soviets, they concentrated on **unmanned** missions to the Moon to obtain samples of lunar **soil**. In 1970, they sent a probe to Venus. On July 1975, another historic event took place. *Apollo 18* and *Soyuz 19* linked up at a "special" rendezvous. Americans and Soviets met in orbit, sending a message of peace back to Earth.

soil: dirt and earth.

unmanned: without astronauts on board.

APOLLO II CREW

APOLLO – SOYUZ RENDEZVOUS

MIR

Chapter V

Skylab was the first space station put into orbit, in 1973. In 1977, the Soviet space station *Salyut 6* was launched and its **crew** members were from Czechoslovakia, Poland, Germany, Bulgaria, Hungary, Vietnam, Cuba, Mongolia and Romania. The Soviets replaced it with the station *MIR* in 1986.

The Americans made history again in 1981. They launched the first Space Transportation System (STS-1) also known as the space shuttle *Columbia*.

SPACE SHUTTLE

CANADARM

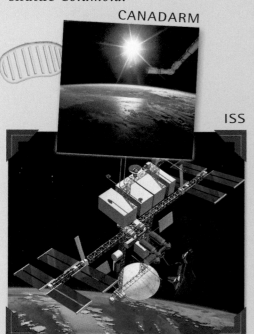

ISS

Chapter VI

In the 1980s, European countries, Japan and even China joined the USSR and USA in space exploration. In Canada, the *Canadarm* was designed for use in American space shuttles. Finally, all nations joined in at the end of the 20th century to build the *International Space Station* (ISS).

By 2005, four Canadians had already travelled in space. Julie Payette is one of them. She served as a mission specialist on the space shuttle *Discovery* from May 27 to June 6, 1999.

After reading and listening

5. **Compare** your chapter titles with a classmate.

6. **Choose** the best titles and present them to your other classmates.

7. Which chapter did you find the most interesting?

8. Which chapter did you find the least interesting?

▼ Reinvest

9. Scan the chapters for important events and dates.

10. Create a timeline of those events.

11. Present your timeline to your classmates.

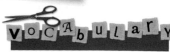

crew: team.

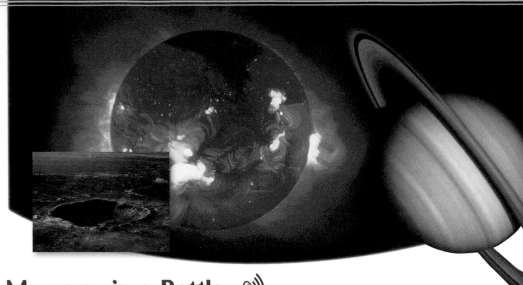

Did you ever send a message in a bottle while playing by a river or by the sea? Did you hope someone would find it and answer back?

Before Reading

1. What is the use of space probes?

2. What kind of information do they send back to Earth?

Reading

3. **Read** the text on the Voyager space probes.

Message in a Bottle 📢🎵

There are two Voyager probes presently somewhere outside our solar system. Voyager II left in August 1977 and Voyager I in September 1977. They were named in the order they would arrive at their first destination: Jupiter. Voyager I was given a shorter trajectory and it arrived at Jupiter first. Their mission was identical though: to explore our solar system.

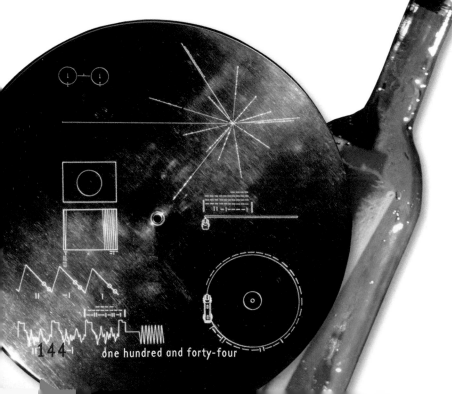

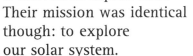

Each Voyager craft carries a kind of message in a bottle. Each one has a thirty centimetre gold-plated disk mounted on one of the sides. The disk contains lots of information about the Earth. It is intended to tell other life forms where and what Earth is. Instructions are written on its protective aluminium jacket to explain how to listen to the recording.

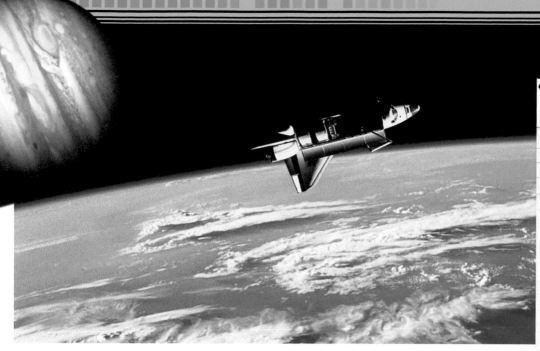

Reading *(continued)*

4. Pay attention to the content of the "message in a bottle".

After Reading

5. Do you think the images, sounds and music they put on the disk are representative of Earth?

6. Do you think someday an alien life form may look at and listen to the disc?

What is recorded on the disk?

115 images such as: The Earth, diagrams of a human male and female, trees, fish, birds, sand dunes, Mars, Mercury, the Sun, seashore, etc.

35 different sounds: whales singing, a kiss, a baby laughing, chimpanzees, rain, surf, life signs such as an electrocardiogram, footsteps, heartbeats, etc.

27 musical selections: from Bach to Mozart to Chuck Berry singing *Johnny B. Goode*, and music and songs from different cultures around the world.

Finally, it includes greetings of welcome in **55 different languages** from Akkadian to Wu.

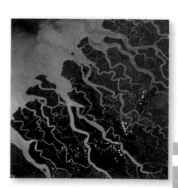

▼ Reinvest

7. Together with teammates, **find** three or more objects you would have put on Voyager's disk.

8. Share your ideas with another team.

Letters to the

STEP 4

In your opinion, is space exploration useful or useless? Is it important or not?

Before Reading

1. **Skim** the letters.

2. What kind of letters are they?
   - letters to a friend;
   - letters of complaint;
   - letters of opinion.

Reading

3. **Read** the letters.

4. On your handout, **identify** a key sentence that represents the opinion expressed in each letter.

◼ Letter A

Dear Editor,

I read an article last week about the dozens of satellites and hundreds of pieces of debris floating in orbit. I think that we will soon be in very big trouble. Don't you agree that everywhere we go, we pollute?

A faithful reader.

◼ Letter B

Dear Ed.,

I don't think we need to colonize space at all. Is it so important that we have a hotel to spend vacations at, on the Moon? A scientific base would be enough. Let's use the money to help people in need.

Y.T.

◼ Letter C

Dear Editor,

I think the International Space Station is a beautiful project for promoting peace, cooperation and solidarity. Weapons and military satellites in space should be banned forever!

A 13-year-old reader

Editor

●●●●●●●●●●●●●●●●●●

After Reading

5. Which letter best reflects your opinion on the subject?

▣ Letter D

Dear Editor,

Why should we visit other planets in our solar system? We should take better care of what we have and forget about space. I think we do not need to waste money and energy on something so far away.

J.D.

▣ Letter E

Dear Editor,

Some people think that the planets of Mars or Venus could be used to get rid of our trash. They think these planets are useless. In my opinion, we should take care of our good Earth and also protect other planets instead of polluting them.

A space-ecology reader

▼ Reinvest

6. With the help of your handout, **write down** your opinion about space exploration.

VOCABULARY

faithful: loyal, constant.

to get rid of: to be free of, to throw away.

useless: having no use.

to waste: to use thoughtlessly, without care.

weapon: device used for fighting or killing such as bombs, firearms, knives, etc.

Project A
Getting Started

Science fiction movies and novels often talk about space tourists. Do you think we will some-day see newspaper ads about space trips?

Before reading

1. **Scan** the text to find what the destinations are in the ads.

2. Are these realistic ads or science fiction ads?

Reading

3. **Read** the ads.

4. **Find** your favourite ad.

STRATEGY

See **Scan,** p. 192.

Space Tourists

□ ■PUBLICITY A

| Send | Reply | Forward | New | Get mail | Mail boxes | Delete |

Spend a day in orbit on the

SUNRISE SHUTTLE.

See the Earth like you never did before. Beautiful views, large shuttle windows and great food. The perfect family trip.

Buy your tickets quickly, only a few seats still available*.

* People interested will have to do one week of **weightlessness** training at their expense.

□ ■PUBLICITY B

Tired of flying only around the Earth?

Come to the Sea of Tranquility, on the Moon!!!

Imagine spending a week by the historic site of the first lunar landing in a beautiful five star hotel. First rate service, indoor and outdoor pool, golf course, a beautiful view of Earth and much more.

What a place for a honeymoon!!

IT'S COOL TO BE A MARTIAN.

Make a stopover on the Moon. Fly through the asteroid belt. Zoom past Phoebus and Demos, the moons of Mars.

Once on Mars, be prepared to be dazzled by everything you see. The Red Desert Hotel built under a dome of multi-coloured plexiglass is waiting for you.

After reading

5. Which ad do you prefer?

6. Which destination would you have chosen?

7. **Find** a slogan for your favourite ad.

CULTURE

Dennis Tito, an American billionaire, was the first space tourist. He paid $20,000,000 to spend six days in the International Space Station in May 2001.

Vocabulary

dazzled: surprised, impressed.

honeymoon: a trip or vacation taken by a couple who have just been married.

weightlessness: a state free of gravity (as in outer space).

▼ Reinvest

A Space Trip Ad   PROJECT A

How about creating your own space trip ad? In this project, don't forget to include:
• A slogan;
• The date of the ad;
• An interesting destination;
• Some descriptions to make the destination more interesting.

Project B 📄
Getting Started

Do you read science fiction comic books? Are you intrigued by the imagination of science fiction writers?

Before Reading

1. **Look at** the pictures in the squares.

2. What is the setting of the story?

3. How many characters are there in the story?

Reading

4. **Read** the story and dialogue.

v o c a b u l a r y

busted: broken.

> Boy, are we in trouble!!

> WE!! It's your fault. YOU were driving.

> Maybe, but who was listening to his new holodisk instead of looking at the instrument panel as he was supposed to?

> I was. But you should have kept your eyes ahead instead of on my holodisk.

> Great. Now it's **busted**.

> BBBBBRRRRRRLLLLL

> Did you feel that?

> Feel what?

> The vibration.

> No.

> I was right, it's **busted**.

> B B BBRRLLL

> There it is again. Did you hear it that time?

> Not your holodisk!!!

> Yeah, I did. It sounds strange but familiar.

> CRR CR RR CRF

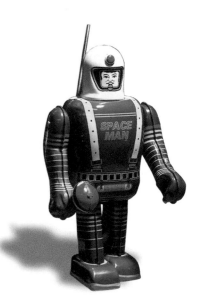

● ● ● ● ● ● ● ● ● ● ● ● ● ● ● ●

After reading

5. Team up with a classmate.

6. Choose a character.

7. With your classmate **act out** the story.

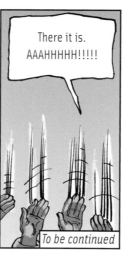

To be continued

▼ **Reinvest**

A Space Story   **PROJECT B**

Choose one of these endings for the story or invent an ending yourself.

1. It's another space ship that picked up their automatic distress signal and has just arrived to save them.

2. They are in the space camp. They got so carried away with their training that they forgot where they were.

In teams, **invent** the dialogue for one ending and finish the strip or act it out.

Space History

Timelines can include different data on the same subject: history, discoveries, science, science fiction books or movies, etc.

Before reading

1. **Look at** the timeline.

2. How many centuries are included?

3. **Scan** the history capsules (A, B, C etc.) for dates.

4. Are they in chrono-logical order?

Reading

5. **Read** the capsules.

6. On your handout, **place** the capsules in the correct order.

After reading

7. Which capsule do you find the most interesting?

8. What type of historical data do you prefer?
   • important events;
   • great people;
   • important inventions;
   • space discoveries.

2000

1900

1800

1700

1600

1500

A) In the early 20th century, French filmmaker Georges Mélies produced a film based on the novel by Jules Verne: *From Earth to the Moon.*

B) The astrophysicist Edwin Hubble was born in Missouri in 1889. The space telescope that bears his name was put into orbit 101 years after his birth.

C) The German engineer Werner Von Braun was born in 1912 and was one of the principal artisans of the American space program between 1950 and 1975.

D) It was Copernicus who published a book in 1543, explaining that the Earth circled the Sun and not the other way around.

E) Galileo's 1609 invention, the telescope, caused a real revolution in the study of astronomy.

F) Christa McAuliffe, a high school teacher and passenger on the *Challenger* space shuttle, died when the shuttle exploded 72 seconds after liftoff in January 1986.

G) Born in 1656, Edmund Halley, a British astronomer, predicted the trajectory and passage of a comet, which was later named in his honour. Its average orbit is 76 years. The last time it was seen was in 1985. The next time it passes by will be in 2061.

H) In 1950, Hergé published the adventures of Tintin on the Moon entitled *Destination Moon* and *Explorers on the Moon.*

▼ Reinvest

A Space Travel Timeline   PROJECT C

Create your own space timeline using information you find in this unit and in other ressources (books, encyclopaedias, Internet). In creating your timeline, don't forget to include the important dates and short descriptions of the events, the people or the discoveries. Verify your data and present your references.

Your Project Presentation

- Did you work individually or in a team?

- If you teamed up, what tasks were you responsible for?

- How much time did you spend on your project?

- What type of material are you planning to use in your presentation? A poster, a skit, a multimedia presentation, etc.

- What were the easiest and most difficult tasks in your project?

- Do you need more practice?

It's time to present your project.

Think of what you want your audience to remember once it has been presented.

Your Portfolio

During this unit, you collected a lot of information about space exploration and space history. You learned to use some new words and expressions; you learned to use new strategies when interacting orally, or reading and listening to texts.

Be sure to put the following items in your portfolio:

- The *In this Unit* handout, to self-evaluate your learning in relation to oral interactions, texts and strategies.

- All the notes and short texts you wrote in the Reinvest section at the end of some of the activities.

- The *Vocabulary* and *Language* handouts that you completed.

- The *Evaluation* handouts you completed.

- Any texts, documents, pictures or handouts that can help you present your project.

Aluminium foil can be so thin that 0.68 kg of this metal is enough to encircle the Earth.

Yelling for 8 years, 7 months and 6 days produces enough energy to heat one cup of coffee.

It is impossible to sneeze with your eyes open.

Every day, people living in the United States eat the equivalent of 22 football fields of pizza.

Fingernails grow nearly 4 times faster than toenails.

1. **Read** these headlines.

2. Are these statements *true* or *false*?

Beetles taste like apples,
wasps like pine nuts
and worms like
fried bacon.

A "jiffy"
is an actual
unit of time
equal to 1/100th
of a second.

- learn and reflect on the curiosity of people about special events and facts;

- discover many unusual and incredible facts;

- criticize the authenticity of news items and facts;

- reflect on the impact of the media on our perception of reality.

Text Types

Look at, read and/or listen to...

a biography, magazine and newspaper articles, fantasy, fiction, science fiction, "how to" texts and instructions, a summary.

Key elements related to articles: headline, byline and lead paragraph.

Strategies

- compare;

- infer with visual clues and contextual cues;

- skim.

Projects

Write or produce one of the following projects:

- *Amazing Facts Magazine;*

- *A School Record;*

- *An Unbelievable Story.*

Illusion or Magic?

●●●●●●●●●●●●●●●●●●
Activity 1

When magicians make people disappear, is it real or is it a trick?

1. Read the short texts.

2. Do you think these tricks involve illusion or magic?

3. Share your answers with your classmates. See **Talk About It**.

A. Houdini and his Escapes

One of Houdini's famous tricks was to put on a strait-jacket and chains and be suspended from a crane. He always managed to free himself.

B. Copperfield and Disappearing Buildings

One of David Copperfield's most famous tricks was when he made the Statue of Liberty vanish. He has also walked through the Great Wall of China. He can also fly!

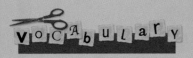

crane:

strait-jacket:

to vanish: to disappear.

STRATEGY

See **Compare**, p. 188.

C. Rabbit in the hat

Can they really make rabbits or pigeons come out of hats? They were wearing it coming on stage. How do you think they do it?

D. Sawing a Person in Two

Many magicians can saw a person in two. They even separate them and push the parts away. How can this be?

E. Sword Tricks

Another classic trick is to insert a sword into a box containing a fragile object like a balloon. Shouldn't the balloon pop?

"A man a plan a canal panama" is the same spelled backwards!

When you share information with classmates, use affirmative or negative statements.

Affirmative	Negative
I think it's an illusion.	*I don't think* it's a magic trick.
My classmate thinks it's real.	*My* other *classmate doesn't think* it's real.

TALK
ABOUT IT!

Can you Trust your Eyes?

With **2D** and **3D** special effects, computers allow us to create and modify real images at **will**.

1. **Look at** the pictures on this page.

2. Which are real? Which are modified?

3. What makes you think that these pictures are real or modified with special effects?

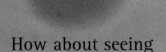

How about seeing the sound barrier?

Do you feel safe in your bus?

VOCABULARY

2D, 3D: abbreviation for two dimensions and three dimensions.

brain teaser: a mentally challenging problem or puzzle.

to stare: to look long or hard at something or someone.

at will: as much as someone likes.

How about some surfing?

Watch out! It's hot!

TYPEWRITER is the longest word that can be spelt using the letters on the first row of a "qwerty" keyboard.

See **Infer with visual clues,** p. 191.

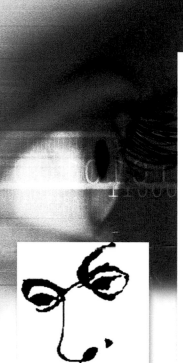

A) Is it a face or a word?

B) Stare at this image. What happens?

4. **Look at** the images on this page.

5. **Answer** questions A, B, C and D.

6. **Find** a name for these kinds of images.
   • special effects;
   • optical illusions;
   • **brain teasers.**

C) Does this make sense?

YELLOW BLUE ORANGE
BLACK RED GREEN
PURPLE YELLOW RED
ORANGE GREEN BLACK
BLUE RED PURPLE
GREEN BLUE ORANGE

D) Can you say these colours out loud? Do not read the words.

A Real "Indiana Jones"

Robert Leroy Ripley (1890–1949)

Robert L. Ripley was a journalist and cartoonist. He was very interested in everything bizarre and by unusual facts about our planet.

For him, people, animals, plants and even objects were a source of extraordinary phenomena. During his many trips, he wrote stories, drew cartoons and produced radio and television shows.

During one trip, he covered 39,000 km by air, ship, horse, camel and donkey! He really loved adventure and was always on the lookout for new things to discover. He was extremely curious.

Today, his stories and cartoons are still read by people all around the world. Since his death, other writers and cartoonists have continued his work.

STEP 1

Do you think it's possible to travel the world to meet fantastic people and find amazing things?

Before reading

1. **Look at** the subtitle of the text on this page.

2. **Decide** what type of text it is.
   - biography;
   - journal;
   - story.

Reading

3. **Read** the text on this page.

4. Which paragraph best describes Mr. Ripley?

STRATEGY

See **Infer with contextual cues**, p. 191.

VOCABULARY

camel:

cartoonist: a person who draws cartoons.

donkey:

drew: past tense of the verb *to draw*.

intriguing: interesting.

outrageous: shocking or bad.

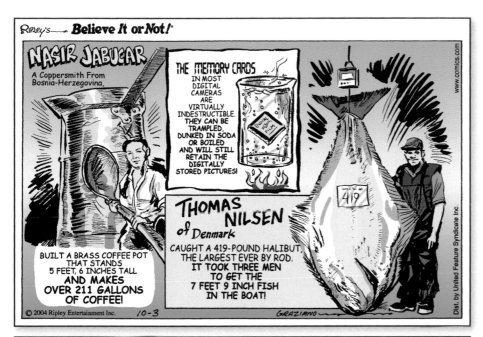

NASIR JABUCAR

A Coppersmith From Bosnia-Herzegovina,

BUILT A BRASS COFFEE POT THAT STANDS 5 FEET, 6 INCHES TALL **AND MAKES OVER 211 GALLONS OF COFFEE!**

© 2004 Ripley Entertainment Inc. 10-3

THE MEMORY CARDS IN MOST DIGITAL CAMERAS ARE VIRTUALLY INDESTRUCTIBLE. THEY CAN BE TRAMPLED, DUNKED IN SODA OR BOILED AND WILL STILL RETAIN THE DIGITALLY STORED PICTURES!

DIGITAL FILM

THOMAS NILSEN of Denmark

CAUGHT A 419-POUND HALIBUT, THE LARGEST EVER BY ROD. IT TOOK THREE MEN TO GET THE 7 FEET 9 INCH FISH IN THE BOAT!

GRAZIANO

www.comics.com
Dist. by United Feature Syndicate Inc.

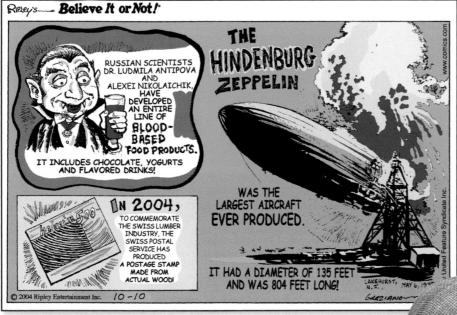

RUSSIAN SCIENTISTS DR. LUDMILA ANTIPOVA AND ALEXEI NIKOLAICHIK, HAVE DEVELOPED AN ENTIRE LINE OF **BLOOD-BASED FOOD PRODUCTS.** IT INCLUDES CHOCOLATE, YOGURTS AND FLAVORED DRINKS!

IN 2004, TO COMMEMORATE THE SWISS LUMBER INDUSTRY, THE SWISS POSTAL SERVICE HAS PRODUCED A POSTAGE STAMP MADE FROM ACTUAL WOOD!

THE HINDENBURG ZEPPELIN WAS THE LARGEST AIRCRAFT **EVER PRODUCED.** IT HAD A DIAMETER OF 135 FEET AND WAS 804 FEET LONG!

LAKEHURST, N.J., MAY 6, 193-

GRAZIANO

© 2004 Ripley Entertainment Inc. 10-10

www.comics.com
United Feature Syndicate Inc.

Reading *(continued)*

5. **Read** Ripley's comic strips on this page.

6. What information is...
   a) ...the most **outrageous**?
   b) ...about a world record?
   c) ...about technology?

After reading

7. What information do you think is the most interesling?

8. Would you say that Ripley's stories are:
   • amusing;
   • serious;
   • **intriguing**;
   • boring.

▼ **Reinvest**

9. Write your own description of Ripley using keywords from the text.
   • What kind of person was he?
   • What were his interests?
   • What did he do?

Very Unique Museums

Do you think that all museums are the same? Have you ever visited an **unusual** museum?

Before Reading

1. **Name** the museums you know or have visited.

2. **Look at** the pictures and the titles.

3. Would the objects in those pictures be shown in one of the museums you know?

Reading

4. **Read** the articles.

5. Where are these museums located?

After Reading

6. Which of these museums would you like to visit?

7. Do you think a museum has to be "serious" to be interesting?

The Toilet Museum

In New Delhi, India, you can visit a toilet museum. Discover the history of toilets. Who were the first users? How did technology help humans get rid of one of the oldest problems in the world?

The Dirt Museum

In Boston, USA, you can stop by the dirt museum. You'll see tons of jars filled with all kinds of dirt from around the world. From Antarctica to Beverly Hills and also dirt from the Great Wall of China, we **dare** you to name a place from which we don't have a piece of dirt in a jar.

Great Wall of China

The Toaster Museum

In Charlottesville, USA, you can now visit a museum about what you use in the morning: the toaster. From the first ever invented to the most modern toasting technology, everything is there. You thought toasting was a light subject, but just talk about it to the people at the museum.

VOCABULARY

to dare: to challenge.

unusual: uncommon or different.

CULTURE

The Ashmolean Museum in Oxford, England is the world's first and oldest university museum. It opened in 1683.

▼ **Reinvest**

8. **Create** a poster or a commercial to advertise one of these museums.

Funny Laws

In Canada

The criminal code has a clause that forbids people to smell in public!

In Richmond, Virginia, USA

It is illegal to flip a coin in a restaurant to see who pays for a coffee.

In Alaska, USA

It is considered an offence to push a live moose out of a moving airplane.

STEP 3

Some laws have not been changed in a very long time. Maybe some of us are breaking these laws without knowing it? Watch out!

Before reading

1. **Look at** the illustrations.

2. Where does each law come from?

Reading

3. **Read** the texts.

4. Do you think these laws make sense?

After reading

5. In your opinion, which of these laws should be abolished?

VOCABULARY

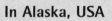

code: a set of rules and regulations.

smell: odour or scent.

▼ Reinvest

6. **Team up** with a classmate.

7. Write your own funny law:
   - choose an ordinary event from life or a very unique occasion;
   - make it illegal by writing out a "legal" text.

8. **Share** your new law with the rest of the class.

WRITE ABOUT IT!

It is forbidden to... ▢.

It is illegal to... ▢.

Where in the World...?

STEP 4

Nature is filled with amazing animals and phenomena. What is the most special thing in nature that you can think of?

Before Reading

1. **Skim** these two pages to identify the animals.

2. **Tell** on which continent they live.

Reading

3. **Read** the information in the boxes.

4. In your opinion, in each case, is the information true or false?

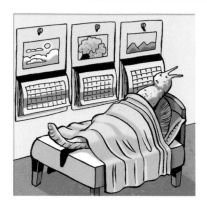

A) Snails can sleep for three years.

B) Camels have three eyelids to protect them from blowing sand.

Hmmm! Not bad.

C) Butterflies have about 12,000 eyes and taste with their hind feet.

A Genuine Fact

It is easier for a left-handed person to open a jar than a right-handed person. This is because a left-handed person can apply a stronger anticlockwise movement.

D) Almost all polar bears are left-handed.

E) The elephant is the only mammal that cannot jump.

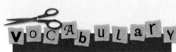

After Reading

5. Which piece of information do you find the most surprising?

G) The Kakapo is the world's heaviest parrot. It cannot fly because it is too fat. Some weigh over 3.6 kg.

F) A giraffe can clean its ears with its 53 cm tongue, but it has no voice.

vo**c**A**b**u**l**a**r**y

eyelid:

hind: located at the back, posterior.

▼ Reinvest

6. In teams, **find** out a special fact about an animal or a plant you know.

7. Write **down** this special fact. ✐

8. Draw or **find** a picture to illustrate your special fact.

Astonishing News!

Project A
Getting Started

Articles and news items are written to catch the eye. What catches your attention when you read a newspaper or a magazine?

Before reading

1. **Skim** these pages.

2. **Find** the headlines, bylines and lead paragraphs. See **Write About It**.

Reading

3. **Read** all the items.

4. **Match** the correct headlines, bylines and lead paragraphs in order to put the three articles together correctly.

A A prehistoric teenager chewed it 9,000 years ago

B
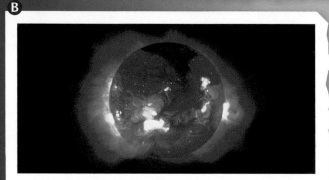

The Sun is some 333,400 times more massive than Earth and contains 99.86% of the mass of the entire solar system. That means that the nine planets and their moons, and the asteroid belt all put together only make up about 0.14% of the Solar System's mass.

C The oldest known sample of gum was found near Ellos, Sweden in 1993. The well-chewed gum, made from honey-sweetened resin, contained tooth marks that, amusingly, appeared to be those of a teenager.

D The Sun, 99% of Solar System's Mass

E It happened for the last time on March 28th, 1848

F Niagara Falls, about to Freeze

STRATEGY

See **Skim,** p. 192.

WRITE ABOUT IT!

A magazine or newspaper article includes a **headline**, a **byline** and a **lead** paragraph.

The **headline** is the title of the article.

The **byline** completes the headline by providing a significant detail.

The **lead** paragraph relates the key information.

After reading

5. Why do you think headlines must be written like that?

6. Why are headlines, bylines and lead paragraphs printed with different **fonts**?

G Oldest Chewing Gum in Exhibition

H

The flow of water was stopped completely over both falls on March 29th, 1848 due to an ice jam in the upper river for several hours. This is the only time it is known to have occurred. The falls did not actually freeze over, but the flow was stopped to the point where people actually walked out and recovered artefacts from the riverbed!

VOCABULARY

exhibition: a public presentation or showing.

font: a style of printed letters, signs or numbers.

sample: small piece.

several: more than two or three but not many.

I Scientists Determine the Precise Density of the Sun

▼ **Reinvest**

 **Amazing Facts Magazine** | **PROJECT A**

When you create your *Amazing Facts* article, don't forget to include:
• a headline, byline and lead paragraph;
• pictures or drawings.

An Official School Record

What do the oldest person in the world, the tallest tower in the world and the longest paper clip chain all have in common?

They hold the world records for being the oldest, the tallest and the longest!

Project B
Getting Started

Do you think breaking a record is a complicated thing to do? Do you know how to organise a record-breaking activity?

Before reading

1. **Skim** pages 168-169.

2. What is PART 1 about?
   • a "how to" guide;
   • a letter;
   • a questionnaire.

3. What is PART 2 about?
   • a "how to" guide;
   • examples of records;
   • a newspaper article.

Reading

4. **Read** PART 1.

5. What is the name of the section where you find a summary of PART 1?

PART 1 **HOW** to organize a record-breaking activity:

❶ You need to decide what you would like to do. Remember that it must be something fun, safe and inexpensive.

❷ You need to make a list of the materials (if any) that you will need to break the record.

❸ Make sure you have the school's permission to use the school grounds, rooms and equipment.

❹ Set a date and ask people from your school to come and participate or watch and **cheer** you while you try to set or break your world record.

❺ Be sure to have video or photographic proof that you set or broke your record.

Ask yourself these questions:
• Do I need a lot of space?
• Do I need people to participate? How many?
• Do I need special equipment?

vOCABuLArY

to cheer: to encourage.

to shuffle: to mix playing cards.

skill: ability.

stack: a pile of things on top of each other.

In other words

Do something...	Don't do anything...
...safe	...dangerous or against school rules
...fun	...disrespectful
...measurable or countable	...beyond your capacity
...cheap	...too expensive
...provable and breakable	...that is impossible for you to break

PART 2

WHAT type of record can you try to break?

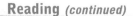

Here are a few examples:

A) Tallest coin column

You'll need stacks of patience – and stacks of cash – if you want to build the world's biggest stack of coins.

B) Most eggs held in the hand

You'll need "eggs-traordinary" skills – and big hands! How many eggs can you hold in your hand at once?

C) The longest paper clip chain or conga line

You'll need either a very big box of paper clips or a lot of your friends to break these records.

D) Speed gift-wrapping

Have Christmas all wrapped up in no time with this speed record attempt. How quickly can you gift-wrap a present?

E) Fastest card arranging

Take a deck of playing cards that has been shuffled a few times. Against the clock, arrange them back in numerical order.

Reading *(continued)*

6. Read PART II.

7. Which of the examples would you like to try?

8. Is each of the examples acceptable according to the guidelines in PART I?

After Reading

9. What kind of record would you like to beat?

10. Do your ideas follow the guidelines?

 Reinvest

 **A School Record**   **PROJECT B**

When you organize your own record-breaking event in your school, don't forget to:
- follow the guidelines;
- plan everything you need to set a record;
- ask your teacher to help you make your record official.

Incredible Hoaxes

Project C
Getting Started

Do you know that some stories are so incredible that a lot of people believe them? Do you think that the media is easy to **fool**?

Before Reading

1. **Look at** the pictures and the titles.

2. What are the articles about?

Reading

3. **Read** the articles.

4. Why do you think these hoaxes worked?
   - because they looked true and real;
   - because the media promoted them.

After reading

5. Which of these two hoaxes do you prefer?

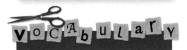

to cheat: to act dishonestly, to be dishonest.

to fool: to trick someone; to pretend.

hoax: a story or trick meant to **fool** people.

to sweat: to perspire.

ROSIE RUIZ
WINS THE BOSTON MARATHON

On April 21, 1980, Rosie Ruiz won the Boston Marathon in the women's category. At the finish line, she was not even **sweating**. Also, nobody could remember seeing her during the race.

Some people told race officials that she may have entered the race in the final few meters. In fact, she had only run the last part of the race. After the fact, people discovered she also **cheated** at the New York Marathon where she rode the subway to win the race.

The War
of the Worlds

On October 30, 1938 the radio was broadcasting a musical program. The music was suddenly interrupted by a news report saying that a blue meteor was coming towards Earth. Minutes later, it was announced that it had crashed and that Martians were coming out of it and attacking people.

People listening to the radio thought it was real. The phone lines were busy and people started buying provisions to survive the attack. After a while, everyone learned that it was only a theatre play on the radio written and produced by Orson Welles and the Mercury Theatre.

▼ **Reinvest**

 **An Unbelievable Story**

PROJECT C

To prepare and write your **hoax** news item or story, don't forget to:
- use anything that comes to your mind, even if it's unbelievable;
- make the story appear real (visual and text).

Your Project Presentation

- • Did you work
  individually
  or in a team?

- • What type of sources
  did you use to find
  information?

- • Did you ask your teacher
  to validate your project
  and topics ?

- • How much time did you spend
  on your project?

- • Did you revise the written
  part of the project?

- • What were the easiest and
  most difficult tasks in your project?

It's time to present your project.

Make sure your audience has polished
documents so everyone understands
your work.

Your Portfolio

During this unit, you read many texts
related to special facts including magic
and illusion, special effects, hoaxes, etc.
You learned to use some new words and
expressions; you learned to use new strategies
when interacting orally, and reading or
listening to texts.

Be sure to put the following items in your
portfolio:

- • The *In this Unit* handout, to self-evaluate
  your learning in relation to oral interactions,
  texts and strategies.

- • All the notes and short texts you wrote in
  the Reinvest section at the end of some of
  the activities.

- • The *Vocabulary* and *Language* handouts that
  you completed.

- • The *Evaluation* handouts you completed.

- • Any texts, documents, pictures or handouts
  that can help you to present your project.

Toolkit

Reference Toolkit

This part of your Student Book has three sections.

PROCESSES

This section explains how to use the **Response process,** the **Writing process** and the **Production process,** which you need in order to understand, write or produce texts.

STRATEGIES

This section explains how and when to use strategies you need when you communicate and when you learn. Some of these strategies are introduced in the *Strategy* boxes in the Units of your Student Book.

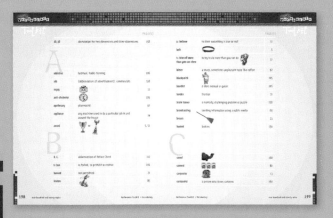

VOCABULARY

This section is a list of all the words found in the *Vocabulary* and *Idiom* boxes in the Units of your Student Book. You will find short definitions and pictures to help you understand their meaning.

Table of Contents

Toolkit

Response process

CONNECT

EXPLORE   GENERALIZE

RESPONSE PROCESS

Use the *Response process* when you **read, listen to** or **view** a text (written text, conversation, dialogue, audio or video documents).

This process will help you understand the meaning of a text through interaction with your teacher and your classmates.

■ Explore

Say what you found most interesting about the text.

Interact orally about:

- the main topic of the text;

- something you discovered;

> I found that the topic is...

> I learned that...
> I discovered that...

- a quote from the author;

- a first impression.

> The author says/tells...

> At first, I noticed that...

Toolkit

Connect

Share with others what it is that connects you to the text.

Interact orally about:

- your own experience or someone else's experience;

> I also…
>
> This reminds me of…

- your feelings;

> This text/that part makes me feel…
>
> I was (curious, sad, afraid of, happy, etc.) that…

- a character;

> Like this character, I…

- something you know about the main topic of the text.

> I remember reading/watching/ listening to…

Generalize

Share your conclusions and opinions about the text.

Express what you think about:

- the characters' actions in the story;

> If this happened to me, I would have…

- the importance of the main topic;

> In my opinion, this text…

- something everyone should be aware of;

> I think we/everyone should…

- the author's point of view.

> I think the author is right/wrong about…

Toolkit

Writing process

WRITE
PREPARE
REVISE
REFLECT
PUBLISH
EDIT

WRITING PROCESS

Use the *Writing process* when you **write** a text.

This process will help you **plan** your writing activities and **reflect** on what and how you wrote.

■ Prepare to write

Before beginning to write, determine your purpose for writing, your target audience and your text type.

A. Discuss and write down your ideas.

- brainstorm with others about ideas and topics;
- activate your prior knowledge of the language to be used and what you know about the topic;

B. Write down an outline of the text.

C. Use various resources to find new information (books, the Internet, media, etc.)

■ Write your draft

Begin to write and focus on the meaning of your text.

A. Use your ideas and your outline.

B. Write down short, complete sentences.

C. Use language and vocabulary you know.

D. Ask for help or advice when needed.

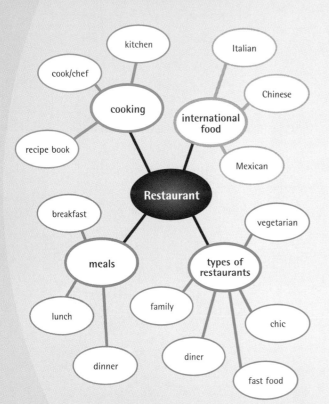

kitchen
Italian
cook/chef
Chinese
cooking
international food
recipe book
Mexican
Restaurant
breakfast
vegetarian
meals
types of restaurants
family
lunch
chic
diner
dinner
fast food

My Favourite Restaurant.

Toolkit

■ Revise your draft

Read what you have written and verify the organization of your ideas.

A. **Read your draft as if you were the target audience.**

B. **Rearrange, clarify and complete your ideas when needed.**

each Friday night.

I rent dvds at the video club in my village. I like to watch a movie.

C. **Double-check your word choice.**

My best friend watches the ~~dvd~~ with me.
movie

D. **Ask for another person's feedback.**

E. **Rewrite your draft with the modifications you made.**

I like to watch a movie each Friday night. I rent dvds at the video club in my village.
My best friend watches the movie with me.

■ Edit your text

Verify your spelling, capitalization, punctuation, sentence structure and language.

A. **Use resources like different models, dictionaries, thesauruses and grammar references.**

B. **Ask for help or advice when needed.**

■ Publish your text

Prepare the final version of your text.

A. **Take into account your text type.**

B. **Make a polished copy.**

C. **Present your text to the target audience.**

Toolkit

Production process

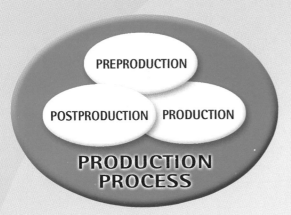

Use the *Production process* when you **create** a media text (poster, video, web page, skit, etc.)

This process will help you **plan** your productions. It will also help you **reflect** on how you produce them and if they fit your needs.

■ Preproduction

Before producing a media text, determine your purpose for producing it, your target audience and your media text type.

Plan all the material you need and the content of your media text as well.

A. Discuss and write down your ideas.

- brainstorm with others about ideas and topics;

- select an appropriate media text type to produce (poster, video, skit, radio show, web page, etc.);

- activate your prior knowledge of the language to be used and what you know about the topic and the media;

- write down your focus sentence;
  We want to produce a poster for our Halloween Party.

Toolkit

B. Use various resources to find new information (books, the Internet, media, etc.)

C. Decide if your media text type is appropriate to your production.

D. Create a script or a storyboard using your ideas.

E. Ask for another person's feedback and make adjustments.

Target audience:

Content:

Things to do:

■ Production

Produce your media text.

A. Use your script or storyboard.

B. Include elements appropriate to your media text type (illustrations, photos, texts, symbols, etc.).

C. Use the writing process if needed (See pages 176–177).

■ Postproduction

Prepare the final version or your media text.

A. Edit and make a polished copy of your media text.

B. Ask for another person's feedback and make any last adjustments.

C. Present your media text to the target audience.

Toolkit

Communication strategies

■ Stall for time

Use this strategy when you need time to think, when you hesitate, or before you answer.

Examples:

Do you like it?

Well, emmm...
Let me think about it...

Are you ready to order?

Give me just one little minute...

■ Recast

Use this strategy to check if you heard the right word.

Simply repeat what you heard.

Example:

What time is it?

It is four-fifteen.

Did you say four-fifteen?

Toolkit

■ Gesture

Use body and facial expressions to help communicate your message.

Use this strategy when:

- you want to help your audience understand your message;
- you are looking for a word;

Examples:

> Where is Mrs. Johnson's office?

> Take the corridor on your left.

> This movie was very scary. I'm not so sure I liked it...

> I loved it! It was great!

Toolkit

■ Rephrase

Use this strategy when you feel your message is not understood.

Use other words to say the same thing again.

Example:

What time does the bell ring?

At a quarter to noon.

At eleven forty-five.

Excuse me?

?!?!

In 5 minutes!

■ Substitute

Use this strategy to simplify your message.

Replace certain words by other words that are less precise, but easier to understand.

Examples:

Are you coming to the library with me?

To where?

Oh! Okay!

To the place with lots of books!

Do you like hiking?

What is hiking?

Walking in the forest.

It sounds like fun!

Learning strategies

■ Direct attention

Focus on your work. Do not let distractions affect your concentration.

Example:

Toolkit

■ Pay selective attention

Use this strategy when you need information concerning precise details.

For example, you could use this strategy when:

• You are getting ready to read or listen to a text.
• You are revising your answers, your project or your text.

Example:

> **Revision Check List**
>
> ✓ singular/plural?;
> ✓ verbs: past or present tense?;
>   title/capital letters;
>   present tense: he/she/it verb + s.

• You are listening to an audio document or watching a video.

Example:

> What is the topic of this video?

> What are the names of the characters?

Toolkit

■ Plan

Think of what you need to do **before** you start your work.

Use this strategy when:

- You are starting a new project.

Example: **Project Planning – What do we need to do for our skit?**

> **A.** brainstorm on the story.
> **B.** write the dialogue.
> **C.** practise the skit.

> **D.** find costumes and other props.
> **E.** practise with props.
> **F.** present the skit to class.

- You are given a deadline.

Example:

February

8th – Brainstorm
9th – Write dialogues
11th – Practise the skit
15th – Find props

■ Self-evaluate

Use this strategy whenever you reflect on what you have learned.

Example:

Things I Need to Practise

1. Take more risks when speaking;
2. Present tense: He <u>doesn't</u> like;
3. More practise before presentation.

My Good Shots

1. Good cooperation with teammates;
2. Accurate planning;
3. I learned many new words.

Toolkit

Self-monitor

Use this strategy whenever you realize you made a mistake.

Correct yourself...

• When speaking:

Example:

> We had some very good kitchen last night for dinner.

> Ooops! I mean... We had very good chicken last night!

> My sister don't like... Sorry! She doesn't like chicken.

> Huhh?!?

• When writing:

Example:

> I sometimes need my dictionary to look up the spelling of certain words.

My Camping Trip to the White Mountains

I went
Last summer, i go camping with my family.

beautiful
It was fantastic! The White Mountains are big and beautifull.

■ Activate prior knowledge

Think of what you already know on the subject.

Connect new information to what you already know.

Use this strategy before:

- reading a text;
- viewing/listening to audio/video documents;
- starting a project;
- expressing your opinion on a topic.

Example:

Will you watch
"The Olympic Games" on TV?

Okay, what do I already know about the Olympics?

sports competitions, medals, diving, racing, countries,
training, perseverance, pride, athletes...

■ Predict

Make hypotheses based on what you already know.

- Guess what the topic of the text/conversation is.

- Guess what will happen in the story.
  Use the information given by the **title, subtitle, illustrations, pictures,** etc.

Example:

Our Dinner With Dracula

■ Compare

Observe and note important similarities and differences.

You can compare many things (words, sentences, expressions, pronunciation, etc.).

Example:

- You can compare two words and their pronunciation.

> I live near my school.

> I leave home at 8:10 every morning.

■ Recombine

Put together small elements you have learned before, in a new way.

Example:

> For this game, we need markers and a dictionary.

> Could you share your dictionary with me? I forgot mine.

> Okay. Could you share your markers ?

■ Delay speaking

Take time to listen and then speak when you feel ready.

Example:

> *You have to be <u>careful</u>.*

> My friend just said that word....
>
> CARE-ful.
>
> OK, I am ready to speak now.

> How do we pronounce that word?

Toolkit

■ Practise

Apply what you learned to other situations.

Example:

In class

May I help you?

I would like a ham sandwich, please.
Do you have any chocolate milk?
How much does it cost?

In everyday life

Hello, may I help you?

Yes. I would like to try
these shoes on.

Do you have size 6?
How much do they cost?

Toolkit

■ **Infer**

Make intelligent guesses using the clues available, such as:

- **with cognates** (words that are similar in English and in French)

Example:

Blue   People who like blue are cool, calm and relaxed. They are confident, intelligent and strong. They are loyal and faithful friends. They like stability. They dislike change and last-minute things. In ancient Rome, public servants wore blue. In China, blue is the colour for little girls.

- **with intonation or patterns**

Example:

Toolkit

• with visual clues or contextual cues

Examples:

▪ Before you choose a book to read.
Look at the cover of the book.

❶ Look at the title and the illustrations on the front cover.

❷ Look for a short résumé on the back cover of the book.

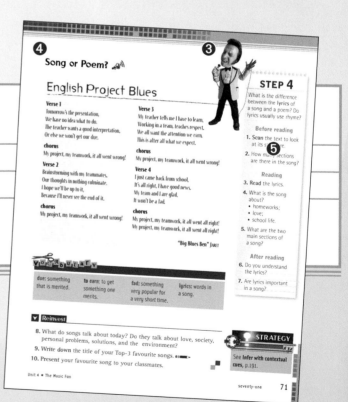

▪ Before you read a text.
Look for the cues.

❸ Look at the illustrations or pictures.

❹ Look at the bigger or darker fonts.

❺ Try to find what kind of text it is (an article, a survey, a fiction text, a riddle, etc.).

Toolkit

■ Scan

Use this strategy when you are looking for specific information in a text.

Look for **keywords** or different types of words.

Example:

Scanning a text can be useful when you are looking for:

- the **name of a place**;
- the **name of a person**;
- an **activity** or a **sport**;
- **dates** and **numbers**.

CULTURE

Most of the movies produced today are filmed in English in their original version. In second place comes movies filmed in Hindi, one of India's official languages. There are nearly 600 movies filmed each year in India.

■ Skim

Read through a text to get an approximate idea of its subject.

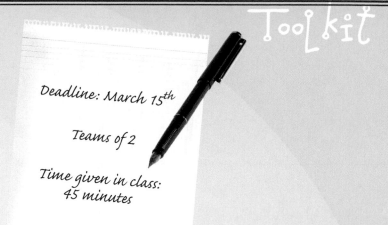

Toolkit

■ Take notes

Write down important information.

This strategy is useful when:

- You are listening to instructions concerning your projects or other tasks:

> Deadline: March 15th
>
> Teams of 2
>
> Time given in class:
> 45 minutes

- You are doing a listening activity or a reading activity:
  - Note the **difficult words** you need to look up in the dictionary;
  - Write down only **keywords** referring to the information you are looking for.
  - Use a **notebook** or **cue cards** to write down your notes.

> Date: Monday, October 15th
>
> ---
>
> Text: A Halloween Legend
>
> Character: Stingy Jack
>
> Storyline: Stingy Jack turns a turnip into a lantern.
>
> Difficult words (dictionary):
> haunt:
> scared:
> coal:
> thought:

- You are brainstorming ideas. See **Use semantic mapping** on the next page.
- You are planning your work. See **Plan** p.185.

Toolkit

■ **Use semantic mapping**

This strategy is useful for brainstorming ideas and grouping ideas in categories that make sense:

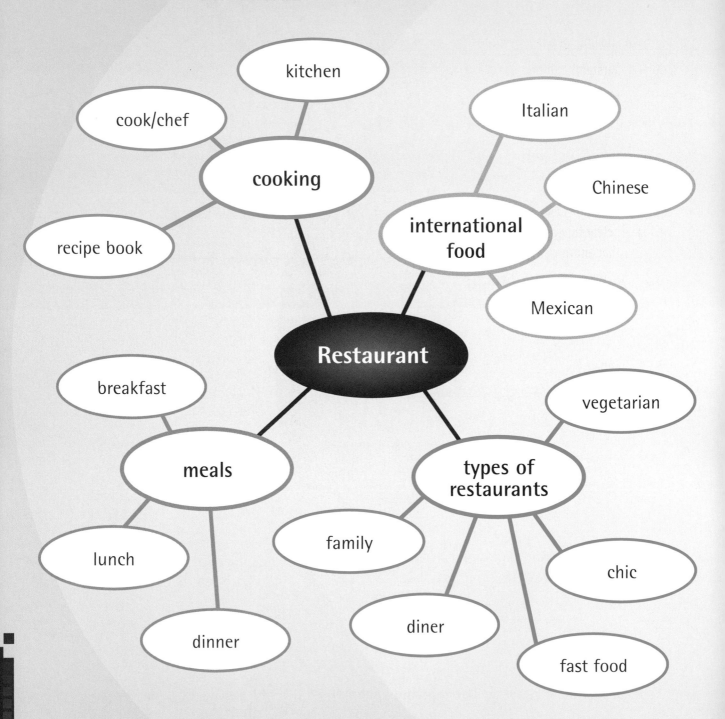

Toolkit

■ **Ask for help, repetition, clarification, confirmation**

Help

Could you help me, please?

I don't understand./I didn't hear very well.

Repetition

Could you repeat slowly, please?

Pardon me. Could you explain this again?

Confirmation

Do you mean…?

Clarification

This is not clear to me. Could you say that another way?

Pardon me. What do you mean by…?

How do we say… in English?

Toolkit

■ Cooperate

Work positively with your teammates by:

- Looking for/sharing ideas;
- Respecting/listening to your teammates;
- Making compromises;
- Participating and working together.

> I have an idea!

> Try your piece of the puzzle this other way...

> Tell us. We are listening to you.

> Great! I placed my piece of the puzzle. Can I help you to place yours?

> I also had an idea, but I think your idea is better.

■ Encourage self and others

Honour pride in your own work and give positive feedback to your teammates.

This strategy is particularly useful when...

- you feel you/your teammate gave your best effort;
- you correct your own mistakes/your teammate corrects his own mistakes;
- you and your team have respected the deadlines and done good work;
- you or a teammate took a risk;
- you or a teammate cooperated well in a task;
- any other positive occasion!

> I gave my best effort!

> I am really proud of myself.

> Thank you! You and I worked very hard.

> You were a great partner. I felt you respected my ideas!

Toolkit

Lower anxiety

Use this strategy in order to be more relaxed when you are dealing with English tasks.

Here are a few tips to help you:

- Take some deep breaths;
- Think of funny/relaxing situations before you have to work;
- Focus on your goals, your objectives;
- Focus on the progress you have made;
- Think of all the resources available to you.

> I can use my dictionary, my personal notes, my teammates, my teacher, the illustrations, my vocabulary section...

Take risks

Take chances and don't be afraid to make mistakes.

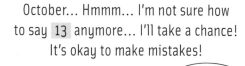

Risking is Learning!
Go for It!

> When is your birthday?

> October... Hmmm... I'm not sure how to say 13 anymore... I'll take a chance! It's okay to make mistakes!

> Yes! Good guess! Thirteen because you are a teenager. I am glad you took a chance.

> My birthday is on October... thirteenth ?... one-three ? Is this how we say it?

Vocabulary Toolkit

2D, 3D	abreviation for two dimensions and three dimensions	158

A

addictive	habitual, habit-forming	106
ads	(abbreviation of advertisement): commercials	118
angry		11
anti-clockwise		109
apothecary	pharmacist	92
appliance	any machine used to do a particular job in and around the house	14
award	or	5, 51

B

B. C.	abbreviation of Before Christ	112
to **ban**	to forbid, to prohibit or restrict	106
banned	not permitted	31
beaten		85

		PAGE(S)
to **believe**	to think something is true or real	11
belt		5
to **bite off more than *you* can chew**	to try to do more than you can do	37
bitter	a sharp, sometimes unpleasant taste like coffee	92
blacksmith		105
booklet	a short manual or guide	105
border	frontier	31
brain teaser	a mentally challenging problem or puzzle	158
broadcasting	sending information using a public media	69
broom		23
busted	broken	150

C

camel		160
canned		80
carpenter		13
cartoonist	a person who draws cartoons	160

to **carve**	to cut or shape something	46
casket		51
celestial	of the sky	139
century	100 years	69
to **cheat**	to act dishonestly, to be dishonest	170
to **cheer**	to encourage	168
cheerful	happy	11
chess		13
Chilean	from the country of Chile	6
choir	a group of singers	61
clockwise		109
code	a set of rules and regulations	163
coffin		47
confectioner	a maker of candies	92
contestant	player	33
couch potato		120
crane		156
craze	something very popular for a short time	72
crew	team	143

PAGE(S)

crooked nose	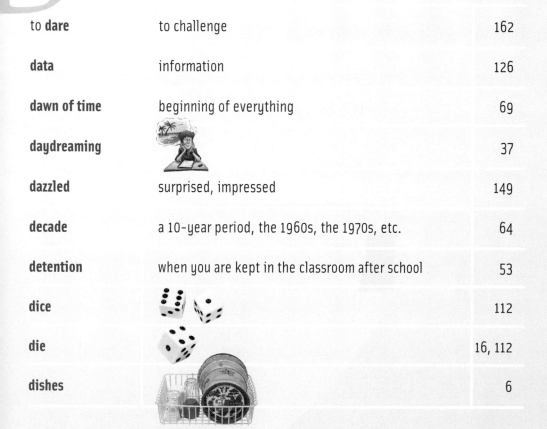	42
crop	vegetables, fruit, cereals or other plants grown in fields	95
crowd	a large group of people	11
cue card		33
to **cure**	to help a sick person get better	92
curly hair		4

D

to **dare**	to challenge	162
data	information	126
dawn of time	beginning of everything	69
daydreaming		37
dazzled	surprised, impressed	149
decade	a 10-year period, the 1960s, the 1970s, etc.	64
detention	when you are kept in the classroom after school	53
dice		112
die		16, 112
dishes		6

PAGE(S)

doll		90
donkey		160
drew	past tense of the verb *to draw*	160
due	something that is merited	71
due to	because of	136
dust	small particles of matter or loose earth	136

E

to **earn**	to get something one merits	71
engine	a motor	141
era	a period of history or time	72
Etruscans	an ancient tribe who lived in Italy before the time of the Romans	95
exhibition	a public presentation or showing	167
eyelid		165

F

		PAGE(S)
fad	something very popular for a very short time	71
faithful	loyal, true; constant	11, 147
far away	at a great distance	23
fast	a period of eating little or no food	90
fasting	eating little or no food	90
feast	a celebration with a lot of food	90
feature	an important characteristic	54
fencing	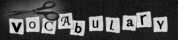	25
fight	battle, conflict	11
to be like a **fish out of water**	to feel out of place, to be in the wrong place	37
to **fit like a glove**	to be exactly right, just what you need	62
font	a style of printed letters, signs or numbers	167
to **fool**	to trick someone; to pretend	170
forbidden	not permitted	27
frivolous	not serious, silly	67
to **fuss**	to worry, to create unnecessary problems	38

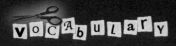

G

		PAGE(S)
garlic		49
to **gather**	to collect	126
gem		105
to **get rid of**	to be free of, to throw away	147
ghoul	an evil spirit	53
gifted	having a special talent	67
glasses		4
glider	an airplane that flies without using a motor	141
glittering	sparkling, shiny	64
a **golden age**	a very important period	73
goose		90
grateful	thankful	90
grave	an excavation in the ground to bury a dead body	47

H

		PAGE(S)
hallway	corridor	37
to **hang out**	to be with friends doing fun things	5
to **hang up**	to end a telephone conversation	102
harvest	gathering the vegetables, fruits or cereals, when they are ready to eat	90
head in the clouds		37
heavens	the sky, space	141
hi-fi	high fidelity, clear sound	69
hiking		25
hind	located at the back, posterior	165
hint	a clue, helpful information	23
hit	a great success	60
hoax	a story or trick meant to **fool** people	170
honeymoon	a trip or vacation taken by a couple who have just been married	149
hood	part of a cloak that covers the head	54
hopeful	optimistic	11

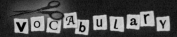
howling	the loud cry of a dog or wolf, especially when in pain	45
huge	very large; big	37, 54

I

icon	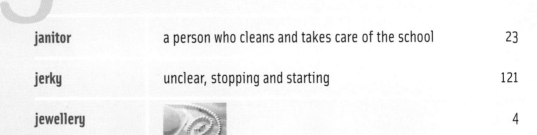	13
indoor climbing		25
inn	a small hotel	105
intriguing	interesting	160

J

janitor	a person who cleans and takes care of the school	23
jerky	unclear, stopping and starting	121
jewellery		4

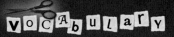

L

		PAGE(S)
ladder		16
lawyer	a person who gives advice or represents other people in court	13
lazybones	an inactive person, someone who sits or lies down a lot	118
leisure	free time, hobby	5
to **lie**	to tell something that is untrue	38
to **litter**		27
lyrics	words in a song	71

M

mashed		85
mess	something disordered, untidy	128
misplaced	in the wrong place	14
to **miss**	to notice that something or someone is lost or absent	24
to **move on**	to do something else	9
to **murmur**	to speak or sing softly	67

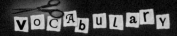

N

PAGE(S)

neat	clean, in order	37
neither... nor	not the one or the other	95
nightmare	a bad dream	47
novel	a fictional story written in a book	136
novelist	a person who writes novels (a story in a book)	136

O

once in a while	sometimes, not very often	123
outrageous	shocking or bad	160

P

parody	a funny imitation	128
pawn		109
to **perpetuate**	to continue something indefinitely	124

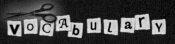

to **picture**	to represent, to describe, to show	124
pinch	a small amout	85
to **plan ahead**	to think about something in advance	38
poltergeist	a noisy ghost	53
to **premiere**	to present something for the first time (a film, a play)	72
prohibited	not permitted	27
propeller		141
proper	correct	14
to **pull in**	to attract	139
to **pump up**	to turn the volume up	61
to **pursue**	to continue	31
quarrel	dispute	11

R

		PAGE(S)
it's **raining cats and dogs**	it's raining a lot, very hard or for a long time	102
rating	evaluation	53
ratings	estimation of the number of people that watch or listen to a TV show, a radio program, etc.	128
reasoning	a way of deciding how things work or what to do next	13
recruit	a new member of a group	139
relationship	a connection between people (family, friends, classmates and people we meet often)	13
relatives	other family members	49
relevant	important, interesting, appropriate	126
reward	something given in return for work, service or effort	106
right-handed	someone who writes with his/her right hand	16
ripe	ready to be eaten	85
in a **row**	one after the other	106
rpm	abbreviation for rotations per minute	69
rule	a statement that indicates what is permitted and what is forbidden	27

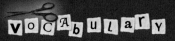
S

		PAGE(S)
sample	small piece	167
schedule	a plan or list of events over time (during a day, a week, a month, etc.)	126
sequel	a movie that continues where an earlier movie ended	51
several	more than two or three but not many	167
to **shuffle**	to mix playing cards	168
significant	important	69
to **sing in key**	to sing on the exact notes	69
skill	ability	168
slave	a person owned by another person	72
smell	odour or scent	49, 163
snake tail		16
soil	dirt and earth	142
that **sounds great!**	it's wonderful!	9
space probe	a device used to explore space	136
squash		90

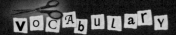

PAGE(S)

stack	a pile of things on top of each other	168
to **stare**	to look long and hard at something or someone	49, 158
stingy	ungenerous	46
stitches		42
strait-jacket		156
string	a thin cord or wire	60
stuffed animal		110
subject	course, *examples:* Math, English, Science, History, etc.	29
supply room	a room used to store paper, products, janitor's equipment	23
to **sweat**	to perspire	170
to **switch places**	to exchange places, to trade places	31

T

to **tag along**	to follow someone	38
takeout		80
thrill	excitement	106

PAGE(S)

through	from one side to the other	136
tip	suggestion	33
tombstone	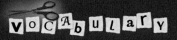	47
tool	any instrument used for doing a job	123
top hat		64
topic	the subject of a text, a book, a discussion, etc.	33
to tour	to travel	67
to train	to get ready for a sports event by repeated practice	128
to trigger	to activate	105
trivia contest	a quiz game	25
truthful	sincere	38
tsp.	abbreviation of teaspoon	85
tube	television	124
turnip		46
twice	two times	80

PAGE(S)

uncanny	strange or particular	29
unmanned	without astronauts on board	142
unusual	uncommon or different	162
useless	having no use	147

to **vanish**	to disappear	156

wallpaper TV viewer	a person who lives with TV as a background to other activities	123
to **waltz**	to dance (a waltz)	64
to **wash away**	to remove, to efface	136
to **waste**	to use thoughtlessly, without care	147
weapon	device used for fighting or killing such as bombs, firearms, knives, etc.	147

PAGE(S)

weightlessness	a state free of gravity (as in outer space)	149
whole	complete, entire	33
whole-wheat		80
at **will**	as much as someone likes	158
wing	section	37
wizard	a magician	105
woes	problems, troubles	37
to **wonder**	to want to know	51

Y

youthful	young, fresh	11

Toolkit

Iconographic references

Rubberball/Firstlight (p. 5 ur) • Carolyn A. McKeone/Photo Researchers, Inc./Publiphoto (p. 7 cl) • NASSIF JEREMIE/CORBIS/SYGMA (p. 12 uc) • Matthias Kulka/CORBIS (p. 18 uc) • LWA-Stephen Welstead/CORBIS (p. 25 dr) • Robert van der Hilst/CORBIS (p. 30 c) • Steve Vidler/SuperStock (p. 31 ur) • Sebastian Bolesch/Alpha Presse (p. 31 ul) • JORGEN SHYTTE/Alpha Presse (p. 31 cl) • Stapleton Collection/CORBIS (p. 64 ur, p. 72 uc) • TPL Distribution Limited/Firstlight (p. 64 c) • LWA- JDC/CORBIS (p. 64 dr) • Bettmann/CORBIS (p. 64 cr, p. 65 ur, p. 65 cl, p. 66 cr, p. 67 u, p. 69 ur, p. 72 cl, p. 72 dc, p. 137 cl, p. 156 ur, p. 156 ul, p. 160 ur, p. 169 dl, p. 170 c) • Lynn Goldsmith/CORBIS (p. 65 cr, p. 66 uc) • Karen Mason Blair/CORBIS (p. 65 dr) • CORBIS/Firstlight (p. 65) • Austrian Archives/CORBIS (p. 67 cl, p. 72 cl) • William Whitehurst/CORBIS (p. 70 ur) • CORBIS (p. 73 cl) • Kevin Schafer/CORBIS (p. 92 r) • akg-images (p. 93 u) • Megapress/Planet Pictures (p. 94 cl) • Search4Stock (p. 102 ul, p. 102 cr, p. 103 ur, p. 103 cl, p. 103 dl, p. 113 c video games) • SuperStock (p. 103 uc) • Megapress/Mauritius (p. 136 dr) • NASA/Science Photo Library/Publiphoto (p. 141 u) • Hulton-Deutsch Collection/CORBIS (p. 141 dc, p. 170 ur) • Reuters/CORBIS (p. 149 dr, p. 156 dr) • NASA (p. 136 cl, p. 137 dr, p. 137 dl, p. 140 ur, p. 140 dr, p. 140 dc, p. 141 c, p. 141 dr, p. 141 dl, p. 142 ur, p. 142 cr, p. 142 dc, p. 143 uc, p. 143 c, p. 143 cl, p. 144 uc, p. 144 cr, p. 144 dl, p. 145 dl, p. 152 ur) • Agence spatiale canadienne (p. 143 dr) • Douglas Kirkland/CORBIS (p. 156 cl) • Bryn Colton/Assignments Photographers/CORBIS (p. 158 ur) • Kurt Jones (p. 158 c) • John McColgan BLM/Alaska Fire Service (p. 158 dr) • Ripley's Believe It or Not!: © United Feature Syndicate, Inc. (p. 161 ul, p. 161 cl) • Chris Andrews Publications/CORBIS (p. 162 dr).